Base
**Rabb.**

# GIFTS from HASHEM

### Arranged for daily study with a "Thought for the Day"

Adapted from *Speak in All His Wonders*
by Rabbi Moshe Goldberger

# GIFTS from HASHEM

Based on the teachings of
Rabbi Avigdor Miller

Adapted from *Speak in All His Wonders*
**by Rabbi Moshe Goldberger**

*Gifts from Hashem*
*by Rabbi Moshe Goldberger*

ISBN: 978-0-9896219-8-4

First Impression .... September 2015

**Published and Distributed by**
Simchas Hachaim Publishing
Copyright © 2015 Simchas Hachaim Publishing
a project of Yeshiva Gedolah Bais Yisroel

**Business Address:**
c/o Yeshiva Gedolah Bais Yisroel • 4 Solond Road • Monsey, NY 10952
Tel (718) 258-7400 x 103 • Fax (718) 258-2394
info@simchashachaim.com

All Rights Reserved

No part of this book of this book may be reproduced in any form — photocopying, or computer retrieval systems — even for personal use, without written permission from the copyright holder, Yeshiva Gedolah Bais Yisroel.

THE RIGHTS OF THE COPYRIGHT HOLDER WILL BE STRICTLY ENFORCED.

Distribution:
U. S.: Simchas Hachaim Publishing
Australia: Gold's World of Judaica 613-9527-8775
Europe: Lehmann's 44-0191-406-0831
Israel: Shanky's 02-538-6936
South Africa: Kollel Bookshop 2711-440-6679

Torah scroll photo: Oleg Ivanov IL / Shutterstock.com

In loving memory of

# Alex and Victoria Missry

# Haim ben Victoria

# Yosef ben Arline

Dedicated by

*The Missry Family*

# The Missry Family Edition

## *Gifts From Hashem*

Dedicated in blessed memory of the
great Gadol of our generation

# Harav Avigdor Miller *zt"l*

whose style of teaching was unique
and influential to generations of
Jews all over the world.

May we all merit to live by his
lessons and follow in his ways.

# Contents

**SHAAR I: THE GIFT OF BECHINAH** .................................................. 15
What Is *Bechina*? ........................................................................ 17
How to Study His Gifts ................................................................ 30
Obstacles to *Bechina* .................................................................. 37
Bechina and Eternity ................................................................... 39
*Bechina* and Loving Hashem ..................................................... 43

**SHAAR II: THE BODY IS A GIFT FROM HASHEM** ........................... 47
Kidneys Are a Gift from Hashem ............................................... 49
Bones Are a Gift from Hashem .................................................. 60
Knees Are a Gift from Hashem .................................................. 66
The Spine Is a Gift from Hashem ............................................... 67
Hands Are a Gift from Hashem .................................................. 68
Feet Are a Gift from Hashem ..................................................... 75
The Mouth Is a Gift from Hashem ............................................. 83
Ears Are a Gift from Hashem ..................................................... 87
Eyes Are a Gift from Hashem ..................................................... 92
Eating Is a Gift from Hashem ..................................................... 98
The Heart Is a Gift from Hashem ............................................... 100
Body Protection Is a Gift from Hashem .................................... 102

| | |
|---|---|
| Teeth Are a Gift from Hashem | 106 |
| Hips Are a Gift from Hashem | 110 |
| The Brain Is a Gift from Hashem | 112 |
| Walking Is a Gift from Hashem | 118 |
| The Liver Is a Gift from Hashem | 119 |
| Skin Is a Gift from Hashem | 124 |
| | |
| **SHAAR III: THE WORLD IS A GIFT FROM HASHEM** | **131** |
| Flowers Are a Gift from Hashem | 133 |
| The Sun Is a Gift from Hashem | 138 |
| Water Is a Gift from Hashem | 141 |
| Rain Is a Gift from Hashem | 142 |
| Thorns Are Gifts from Hashem | 144 |
| The Venus Flytrap Is a Gift from Hashem | 146 |
| Clothing Is a Gift from Hashem | 147 |
| Shoes Are a Gift from Hashem | 149 |
| Wind Is a Gift from Hashem | 150 |
| Eggs Are a Gift from Hashem | 151 |
| Fruits Are a Gift from Hashem | 153 |
| Buds Are Gifts from Hashem | 155 |
| Apples Are Gifts from Hashem | 158 |
| Oranges Are Gifts from Hashem | 162 |

| | |
|---|---|
| Watermelon Is a Gift from Hashem | 163 |
| Dandelions Are Gifts from Hashem | 165 |
| Grass Is a Gift from Hashem | 169 |
| Food Production Is a Gift from Hashem | 171 |
| Your Belt Is a Gift from Hashem | 172 |
| A Hat Is a Gift from Hashem | 173 |
| Seeds Are Gifts from Hashem | 174 |
| Trees Are Gifts from Hashem | 178 |
| Thunder and Lightning Are Gifts from Hashem | 180 |
| Snow Is a Gift from Hashem | 181 |
| Cows Are Gifts from Hashem | 182 |
| Leaves Are Gifts from Hashem | 184 |
| Pollination Is Gifts from Hashem | 187 |
| **SHAAR IV: LIFE IS A GIFT FROM HASHEM** | **189** |
| Mind and Memory Are Gifts from Hashem | 191 |
| Pain Is a Gift from Hashem | 193 |
| Sickness Is a Gift from Hashem | 194 |
| Suffering Is a Gift from Hashem | 195 |
| Poverty Is a Gift from Hashem | 202 |
| History Is a Gift from Hashem | 204 |
| Animals Are Gifts from Hashem | 207 |

## SHAAR V: BEING JEWISH IS A GIFT FROM HASHEM ................. 227
Torah Is the Greatest Gift from Hashem .......................................... 229
Shabbas Is a Gift from Hashem ....................................................... 233
Rosh Chodesh Is a Gift from Hashem ............................................. 241

## SHAAR V: THE MORNING BLESSINGS AND YOUR GIFTS FROM HASHEM ............................................................................................. 243
Why We Say Blessings ..................................................................... 245
"He has commanded us regarding washing the hands…" ........... 247
Asher Yatzar ..................................................................................... 248
Thanking for the Torah .................................................................... 251
"Hashem, the soul which You gave me is pure…" ........................ 253
"Thank You Hashem… for giving the rooster/the mind understanding to distinguish between day and night." ............ 255
"He has not made me a gentile." .................................................... 256
"He has not made me a slave" ........................................................ 257
"He has not made me a woman"/"He has made me [a woman] according to His will." ...................................................................... 258
"He opens the eyes of the blind." .................................................... 260
"He clothes the naked." ................................................................... 261
"He releases the bound." ................................................................. 262
"He raises erect those who are bent over." .................................... 263
"He spreads the earth over the waters." ......................................... 264

"He provides me with all my needs." ............................................. 265

"He prepares a person's footsteps." ............................................ 266

"He girds Israel with strength." ..................................................... 267

"He crowns Israel with glory." ........................................................ 268

"He gives strength to the weary." ................................................... 269

"He removes sleep from my eyes and drowsiness from my eyelids…" …………............................................................................ 270

# Publisher's Introduction

One of the most popular Rabbi Avigdor Miller books was written by a loyal student, Rabbi Moshe Goldberger (based on Rabbi Miller's books and with his approval).

Author of many Torah books and pamphlets, Rabbi Goldberger's *Speak in All His Wonders/Sichu B'chal Nifl'osav*, with the distinctive apple graphic on the cover, has been a perennial favorite of Rabbi Miller readers. Even now, the Simchas Hachaim Publishing office regularly fields calls from readers looking for a copy of "the apple book." *Speak in All His Wonders*, however, had challenges. It was not actually a single book, but three smaller booklets bundled into a single volume (page numbering restarted twice!).

Simchas Hachaim Publishing was grateful when Rabbi Goldberger agreed to allow us to republish his collection in a new, more polished format. In *Gifts from Hashem*, the reader will find his or her favorite thoughts from *Speak in All His Wonders*. The material has been reorganized by general topic and broken into small passages to facilitate short daily readings. Further, the author has added a great amount of new material in the form of a daily thought; thus this edition contains about 30% new content.

The section on the morning blessings has been expanded slightly with material from Rabbi Goldberger's other publications (including *One Hundred Blessings* [Judaica Press]). The complete Hebrew text has been added following the Ashkenaz, Sefard, and Sefardi traditions.

Thank you, Rabbi Miller, for opening our eyes to Hashem's gifts; thank you, Rabbi Goldberger, for allowing us to republish your work!

As always, we must extend our sincere thanks to Yeshiva Gedolah Bais Yisroel. Simchas Hachaim Publishing exists only with the support and encouragement of HaRav Shmuel Miller, *rosh yeshiva*, and Rabbi Yehuda Brog, executive director.

**Aryeh Zev Narrow**
Director
Simchas Hachaim Publishing

# Author's Introduction

Learning the art of *bechina* will change your life.

HaRav Avigdor Miller told me years ago, on a walk, that there are two primary areas that a Jew should focus on in this day and age: the study of Gemara and the study and practice of *bechina*. This will transform our lives. Through *bechina*, we learn how to see the world through the Torah's eyes and how to appreciate Hashem's gifts. We develop an ever-increasing happiness and love of Hashem.

The more we think about His greatness and kindness, the more we thank Him. The more we thank Him, the more we feel His presence in our lives. Learn to thank Him for your life, your family, your eyes, your heart, and your countless other gifts.

The lessons in *Gifts from Hashem* will inspire and fascinate every reader.

**Rabbi Moshe Goldberger**

# Foreword

*"How does one attain love and fear of Hashem? By studying and observing Hashem's creations."*

— Rambam, *Yesodai HaTorah* 2:2

Rabbi Avigdor Miller, *zt"l*, illustrated the importance of realizing the value of the gifts that Hashem has bestowed upon us through the following parable:

Imagine getting a telephone call from the previous owner of your home, who informs you that many years ago, when he lived in your home, he buried a treasure in the basement. Now he is nearing the end of his life and he would like you to have it. All of a sudden you are wealthy! But, in actuality, you were wealthy all along. All you lacked was the knowledge that you owned valuable possessions. It is important to study the unique gifts that Hashem has blessed us with to understand the extent of our wealth.

If you merely browse through these pages, you will not gain the desired effect. Rather, you should pretend that this is a financial report, or your rich uncle's will in which he left you a fortune. Concentrate while studying this report. Consider each item a number of times with deep interest. Tell yourself, "This is amazing and awe-inspiring, and I will therefore sing praise to the Great Designer all the days of my life!"

- Read slowly.
- Review many times.
- Study the actual items with amazement.
- Read a small amount at a time.
- Think it over in your own words and try to add to it from your own understanding.
- Ask Hashem for assistance in viewing His works.
- Share these insights with others.

# SHAAR I
# THE GIFT OF BECHINA

# What Is *Bechina*?

- *Bechina* means to observe and think about the phenomena of the universe in order to appreciate the Creator's wisdom and kindliness.

- The Rambam (*Yesodai HaTorah* 2:2) considers studying Hashem's creations the way to achieve the *mitzva* of loving and fearing Hashem.

- The second chapter of *Chovos Halevavos* is devoted to this subject. It states that this study is the easiest way to develop an understanding and awareness of the Creator.

- "The heavens declare the glory of G-d" (Tehilim 19:2); yet "the Torah of Hashem is perfect" (Tehilim 19:8) because the Torah teaches His ways, His attributes, and His will in a manner superior to the marvels of creation.

- The fundamental principle of the goodness of the world is proclaimed at the beginning of the Torah: "G-d saw all that He had made, and behold, it was *very good*" (Beraishis 1:31).

## THOUGHT FOR TODAY:

When we see something, we can choose to ignore it, or we can choose to appreciate it and thank Hashem for the gift.

# *Mitzvos* You Fulfill when Engaging in *Bechina*

- The *mitzva* of *emunah* (belief): By observing the striking purposefulness of Hashem's handiwork, one becomes much more aware of the Creator.

- The *mitzva* to remember (be mindful) of Hashem: "Lest you forget Hashem" (Devarim 8:11). (Rabbainu Yona, *Shaarai Teshuva* 3:26–27)

- The *mitzva* to meditate in the greatness of Hashem: "You shall know today and put into your heart [mind] that Hashem is G-d" (Devarim 4:39).

- The *mitzva* to remember His kindnesses and to contemplate them: "You shall remember" (Devarim 8:2) and as David said, "The kindnesses of Hashem are in front of my eyes" (Tehilim 26:3).

- The *mitzva* to love Hashem: "By thinking about and enjoying the abundant kindnesses of Hashem, we gain from this comprehension the highest joy, which is the essence of the love of Hashem in which we are obligated" (Rambam, *Sefer Hamitzvos*).

## THOUGHT FOR TODAY:

The word *bechina* stands for *bo chain*, "there is precious charm in it." Everything was created by Hashem with a unique plan and purpose for us to study and appreciate.

# More *Mitzvos* You Fulfill when Engaging in *Bechina*

- The *mitzva* to fear Hashem: "By reflecting upon His wondrous and great deeds and creations, and seeing in them His endless and incomparable wisdom…one will come to love, praise…and fear Him" (Rambam, *Yesodai HaTorah* 2:2).

- The *mitzva* of awareness of Hashem's oneness: By observing that all of creation is united in one purpose — the production and maintenance of life — we become aware of the oneness of the Creator.

- The *mitzva* of *simcha* (joy and happiness): "You shall rejoice with all the good that Hashem has given you" (Devarim 26:11).

- The *mitzva* of *devaikus* (thinking and attaching oneself to Him): "Perfection is to be gained by attachment (*devaikus*) to G-d" (*Mesilas Yesharim* 1).

# THOUGHT FOR TODAY:

We breathe in and out all the time automatically. But why didn't Hashem create us to breathe three times a day and store the air from breakfast until lunch as we do with food?

The answer is to remind us to be aware of His kindness to us in providing air wherever we go.

# More *Mitzvos* You Fulfill when Engaging in *Bechina*

- The *mitzva* of *avodas* Hashem (performing His service): By studying the countless benefits Hashem bestows on a person, one will be humbled and accept upon himself to serve his Creator.

- The *mitzva* of gratitude: It is impossible to have true gratitude unless one studies and is aware of each kindness separately. "How can I repay Hashem for all that He has bestowed on me?" (Tehilim 116:12).

- The *mitzva* to praise Hashem: We are obligated to consider as profoundly as possible the greatness of Hashem and to praise Him accordingly. Because His perfection is endless, our praises, recognition, and expressions of humility of His power and of His kindly attributes should be continuous and everlasting.

# THOUGHT FOR TODAY:

We are obligated to recite one hundred blessings daily, which are expressions of thanks for many of the gifts Hashem keeps on bestowing on us.

For example, we thank Hashem daily for our eyes. You are reading this now with your eyes; thank the Creator for these most perfect cameras!

# *Bechina* Is a Requirement

We are obligated…

- to recognize the countless benefits we receive constantly from Hashem.

- to recognize the *extra* benefits we receive over and beyond that which most people receive.

- to recognize that *all* that is done to us is for our benefit.

- to realize that despite all the intermediaries and apparent causes, everything is really coming to us *solely* from Hashem.

## THOUGHT FOR TODAY:

> Your eyes have color vision. You can look around, see those beautiful, delicious red apples, the orange poster on the wall, the blue sign, and a two-tone colored sefer. Enjoy the colors and thank Hashem.

# Torah Sources for the *Mitzva* to Study Hashem's Kindness and Speak about It Constantly

- "Let me praise Hashem at all times; His praise is always in my mouth" (Tehilim 34:2).

- "Praise Hashem, O my soul, do not forget any of His benefits" (Tehilim 103:2).

- "How numerous are Your works, O G-d; all of them You have made with wisdom (Tehilim 104:24).

- "Speak in all of His wonders" (Tehilim 105:2).

- "All Your deeds praise You, O G-d" (Tehilim 145:10).

- "I shall praise Hashem in my lifetime; I shall sing to my G-d as long as I exist" (Tehilim 146:2).

- "Hashem is good to all, and His mercy is on all His creatures. All Your creatures shall thank You" (Tehilim 145:9–10).

## THOUGHT FOR TODAY:

Why does sound come out of our mouths when we open them? It is a miracle that Hashem opens our mouths and enables us to praise Hashem. We say this as a prayer before each Shemonah Esrai: "Hashem, please open my lips and enable my mouth to relate Your praise."

# More Sources for the *Mitzva* to Study Hashem's Kindness and Speak about It Constantly

- "Raise up your eyes on high, and see Who created these" (Yeshaya 40:26).

- "His greatness and His goodness fill the earth" (Shabbas morning Yotzer).

- "It is good to give thanks to Hashem; to sing to Your name, O Most High" (Tehilim 92:2).

- "This is the duty of all creatures, to thank, extol, praise, and glorify…" (Shabbas morning prayers).

- "What is the way to His love and His fear? When one reflects upon His wondrous, great deeds and creations, and sees in them His wisdom which has no measure and no end, he will surely love and praise…" (Rambam, *Yesodai HaTorah* 2:2).

# THOUGHT FOR TODAY:

When you see a tree with leaves all over your backyard, you are looking at a huge umbrella that Hashem created to provide you with shade to sit under, relax, and enjoy.

You can enjoy the music of birds chirping from the sides, eat some refreshing fruits of the tree, and enjoy Hashem's hospitality.

# How to Study His Gifts

- We are required to study every detail of His kindness, and to spend time speaking of each detail — that is the great function of our lives.

- We fail to recognize His great gifts to us because we become familiar with them: "The frequency of seeing them [the wonders of the universe]...persuade you to discontinue being amazed at them" (*Chovos Halevavos*, *cheshbon* 23).

- We must speak of His kindness constantly to remain aware of it: "Benefit comes from repetition and constant persistence" (*Mesilas Yesharim*, Preface).

- Study of this subject can never be overdone; no matter how much one considers the Creator's greatness and kindliness, it will never be enough. "There is no limit to His greatness" (Tehilim 145:3).

## THOUGHT FOR TODAY:

You cut your skin a few days ago. Hashem has a system of healing powers throughout the body which sent help to repair and heal the wound. If you tore your jacket, it would not sew itself up, but your body does. Thank Hashem!

## How to Study His Gifts (continued)

- All that has ever been said in praise of Hashem barely scratches the surface of this great subject. Since "Hashem founded the world with wisdom" (Yirmiya 51:15), each and every phenomenon demonstrates endless wisdom in each detail's purposefulness and complexity.

- We should always consider the signs of the Creator's wisdom, and we should never cease thinking of them and inquiring about them. One should endeavor to see a new sign (or a deeper perception of a previous observation) every day.

- "When you will reach the limit of your ability, it is proper that you realize that whatever you understand of the wisdom of the Creator and His power in this world is considered nothing in comparison to the truth of His wisdom and power" (*Chovos Halevavos, Bechina* 6).

## THOUGHT FOR TODAY:

Just as Hashem creates the world anew each day for us, we are to study and examine His world constantly to discover some new insight each day.

# True Happiness Comes through *Bechina*

- "Who is wealthy? He who rejoices with his lot" (*Avos* 4:1). The universe is our lot. To cause us to rejoice in it, the Creator declared it *very good* (see Beraishis 1:31).

- By endeavoring to learn the goodness of air, you become a rich man, for there is always plenty of air.

- Feel the goodness of clouds, rain, wind, snow… Enjoy your shoes, clothing, chair, table…

- Be happy with your ability to sleep; rejoice in your strength and energy.

- These possessions are as if they were nonexistent for those who ignore them; only those who are happily aware of them truly possesses them.

# THOUGHT FOR TODAY:

The word *ashir* for wealth can remind us to thank Hashem for our

- <u>A</u>inayim (eyes);
- <u>Sh</u>inayim (teeth);
- <u>Y</u>adayim (hands);
- <u>R</u>aglayim (feet).

These can start us off in thanking Hashem for the grand gift of a billion-dollar body that He bestows on us.

# True Happiness Comes through *Bechina* (continued)

- "Happy is the heart of those who seek G-d" (Tehilim 105:3). A person's happiness and his true success in life depend on his knowing clearly what he seeks.

- The knowledge that he is fully utilizing his life affords him intense satisfaction.

- The pursuit of genuine objectives is intrinsically suited to his spiritual and physical nature, and therefore gives him a foretaste of the ecstasy of the afterlife.

- "The good mind is at an everlasting feast" (Mishlai 15:15). Happiness is not the result of possessions and pleasures, but rather it is the result of proper attitudes of the mind: He who understands the goodness of the world is always rejoicing. Thus the development of these attitudes is actually equivalent to the acquisition of riches.

- The way one learns to look at the world determines the kind of world he will have. Training oneself to live with these thoughts will provide one with a lifetime filled with intense pleasures.

- Through *bechina* a person will become happy, and his entire relationship with the Creator will become a real one. His prayers will be more enthusiastic and his attitude toward the Creator and the ideals of the Torah will be encouraged.

# THOUGHT FOR TODAY:

It's a great error to think that if you had more money you would be happy! Happiness depends on learning to appreciate what you have.

# Obstacles to *Bechina*

- There are three major obstacles we must overcome in order to be able to appreciate the manifold kindnesses Hashem has bestowed and continues to bestow on us.

  - We have been enjoying these benefits from our childhood and we are so accustomed to them so that it is difficult for us to begin feeling grateful for them.

  - People constantly want more than what they have and thus are dissatisfied with what they now possess.

  - There is some suffering in life for each person, thereby causing the constant and countless benefits of life to be overlooked. In order to become aware of the benefits Hashem is constantly conferring upon us, we must reexamine and reappraise all things. By attempting to view all things as if we are seeing them for the first time, we will be able to feel their value and recognize the benefits they bestow. We will also be able to discover that even the apparent sufferings are all blessings in disguise.

- One must beware of those who do not appreciate these truths. One's labor and progress in meditating on Hashem's greatness and His praises will be hampered if one does not avoid the company of fools. Wisdom and understanding do not endure in one who associates with the wicked.

- Effort is required. One must train himself to meditate and concentrate on some objects and processes in the world around us. Even one subject would be sufficient if it were thoroughly investigated and sufficiently emphasized.

## THOUGHT FOR TODAY:

> Hashem created an evil inclination to test us, and He created the Torah to serve as the antidote. Through the Torah and *mitzvos*, Hashem enables us to change how we look at challenges and to control our inclinations. "Who is powerful? One who conquers his inclination" (*Avos* 4:1).

# *Bechina* and Eternity

- The greatest kindness intended by creation is the bestowal upon people of the awareness of the glory of the Creator: "G-d made [the universe] so that they should fear Him" (Koheles 3:14). By gaining fear of Hashem, men gain the greatest benefit in this life as well as gaining eligibility for the true happiness of the World to Come.

- All of the marvelous phenomena of the world a) have manifold physical benefits and b) provide intellectual benefits. These benefits of awareness of Hashem are of primary importance, for they confer on man the Perfection which continues on into the afterlife.

"The foundation of piety and the root of perfect service is a) to make clear and b) to be convinced of what a person's duty is in this world, and toward what he should put his attention in all that he toils all of his days. Our sages have stated that we were created to have joy from being with Hashem… and the true place of this happiness is the World to Come" (*Mesilas Yesharim* 1). By studying *bechina*, we recognize the plan and purpose of the phenomena of creation and we discern the kindliness therein. As we enjoy Hashem's bounty of the universe and sing in gratitude and happiness, we are also rehearsing for the immensely greater future joy which will never end.

# THOUGHT FOR TODAY:

The word *Chumash* (the five books of the Torah) has the same letters as *same'ach*, to be happy. The source of all happiness is through the study of Torah, which is God's blueprint of all of creation.

## *Bechina* and Eternity (continued)

- "In the afterlife there is no eating or drinking...the righteous sit with crowns (of True Knowledge which they gained in this life [Rambam]) on their heads and enjoy the resplendence of G-d's presence" (*Brachos* 17a). The endless joy of the Life to come consists of the ecstasy of viewing the infinite splendor of Hashem's presence; therefore the opportunity to view and appreciate the Creator's splendor in this life is the most important preparation for the great, eternal banquet.

- "Happy are they that sit in Your house," for they "are busy singing in this world" (*Sanhedrin* 91b). After such a life, the best is yet to come: "Still more shall they extol You forever" (ibid.). This life of joy and singing is but a rehearsal for the everlasting career of happy song.

- "This world is like an entrance room before the World to Come; prepare yourself in this world in order to enter the palace" (*Avos* 4:16). "Practice blessing of Him in this world, so that you should be accustomed to them in the World to Come" (*Rashi, Brachos* 63a).

## THOUGHT FOR TODAY:

Why must we sometimes experience "waiting" time or "travel" time? Hashem could have created us so that when we think we want to be in place X, we could be there immediately. The answer is to teach us to use our time are here to *prepare* for the World to Come!

# *Bechina* and Loving Hashem

- The book of Tehilim, which is devoted to teaching the importance of praise of Hashem's wisdom and kindliness, frequently uses the word *hallel* for "praise of Hashem." The *hallel* word denotes an enthusiastic expression of joy and admiration, in a loud and excited manner. We are to train ourselves and our children to get excited in appreciation over the gifts that the Creator is bestowing on us.

- By learning that life is full of happy phenomena, one becomes truly happy. The singing of thanks to the Creator is actually dependent on the study of the joys and benefits of the gifts for which thanks are being given.

- By contemplating and discerning more details of the phenomena and spending more time thinking about them, one understands more clearly these open and astonishing marvels. These testimonies to the Creator's infinite intelligence and benevolence will eventually transform one's life into a career of song of joyous appreciation.

# THOUGHT FOR TODAY:

Being grateful to Hashem is the great secret to wealth.

There is a *mitzva* to count and say at least one hundred blessings every day. Hashem cares for all of our needs. We say in Tehilim 23: "Hashem provides for me, I will not lack." "Who is prosperous? One who rejoices with his portions" (*Avos* 4:1). The more grateful we are, the more we enjoy our riches. The more we thank Hashem, the more we merit to notice and appreciate Hashem's gifts to us.

## *Bechina* and Loving Hashem
### (continued)

- We should also preach to our families and others these teachings about how happy life and all its details are. By mentioning to others the beauty of the scenery and of other creations that Hashem provides, you will stir them to observe these things themselves. By commenting on how enjoyable walking is, or on the exhilaration of deep breathing, or by verbally appreciating a glassful of water, others will take note and also develop these thoughts.

- Opportunities such as Shabbas mealtimes, family travel time, and before bedtime can be utilized as "let us thank Hashem" times. A game can be played in which family members take turns suggesting thoughts of appreciation for which the family should all thank Hashem. (It is surprising to see how many intriguing thoughts of appreciation young children can come up with during these sessions.)

- The same concept has been used in many classrooms (all levels) where the rebbi, teacher, or *moreh* asks the children to suggest items to thank Hashem for, perhaps going through the alphabet and naming something for each letter (e.g., A — apple, B — banana, C — cantaloupe, etc.).

- The study of *bechina* will result in a constant singing to Hashem, in appreciation for the countless benefits we are receiving: "I sing at the deeds of Your hands" (Tehilim 92:5).

- May we merit to fulfill our purpose: "This people I have created for Me, that they relate My praise" (Yeshaya 43:21).

## THOUGHT FOR TODAY:

*Your five fingers can open or close, separate or join together, fold up or stretch out. You can use them as a spoon, fork, cup, knife, hammer, etc. The five-in-one type of knife may have been an attempt to imitate some of the multiple purposes of the fingers and hands that Hashem created for our benefit.*

# SHAAR II
# THE BODY IS A GIFT FROM HASHEM

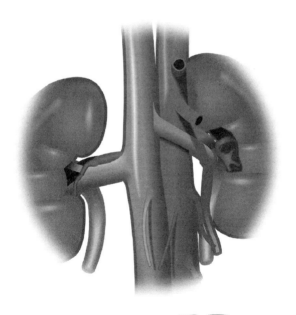

"Thank Hashem for your big gifts…
and they are all big!"

# Kidneys Are a Gift from Hashem

- The Gemara (*Brachos* 61a) defines the role of various organs in the body: "The sages taught: The kidneys advise, the heart understands, the tongue articulates, the mouth [lips] completes the speech process, the esophagus transports all types of food..." First on the list are the kidneys. They are described as giving counsel. Rashi explains they give counsel to the heart. They instruct and the heart understands and chooses to either agree or disagree. The Gemara (ibid.) also teaches the need for two kidneys: One offers positive advice and the other offers negative advice.

- How do we know that the kidneys provide counsel? David Hamelech explains, "I will bless Hashem Who has advised me, even at night my kidneys instruct me" (Tehilim 16:7).

# THOUGHT FOR TODAY:

One of the explanations of how the kidneys instruct us:

Why did Hashem create our blood with the need to be filtered, and then give us miraculous kidneys to perform that function? He could have provided us with blood that always stays clean and pure. The answer is that Hashem is teaching us the purpose of life — to think and choose, to filter our actions, to "turn away from evil and do what is good"!

# Kidneys Are a Gift from Hashem
## (continued)

- The kidneys' function is to provide counsel, exhortations, and *mussar* for which we are to thank and bless Hashem. Rashi explains that the kidneys teach us to fear and love Hashem. This fits well with the next verse, "I set Hashem before me always, He is at my right side, I shall not fall" (*Tehilim* 16:8).

- *Avos D'Rabbi Nasan* (33) and *Midrash Rabbah* teach that the kidney messages are so powerful that they served as the teachers of Avraham Avinu, who had no other *rabbanim* to learn from. They provided him with understanding and counsel sufficient to enable him to reach the spiritual heights that he achieved!

# THOUGHT FOR TODAY:

*The two kidneys serve as a balance, like our two feet, to balance our love and fear of Hashem.*

# Kidneys Are a Gift from Hashem
## (continued)

- How grateful we must be that with all the tasks the kidneys perform, we are generally not even aware that they are functioning! Some 60,000 deaths per year occur in the United States due to kidney disorders, G-d forbid (estimate by the National Kidney Foundation). This number does not include the many (G-d forbid) who must undergo dialysis — an artificial cleansing procedure that may be painful and time consuming — yet less efficient than a healthy kidney.

- In their quiet way, our kidneys are teaching us lessons which we must learn to pay attention to: Just as they function to filter the blood so that the body and mind function smoothly, so too it is our function to do the same on a spiritual level, by filtering out bad character traits.

- The Gemara teaches that taking time to relieve oneself properly is helpful in prolonging one's life (*Brachos* 54b). The Vilna Gaon explains that relieving the body of physical wastes also serves as a parable for eliminating spiritual wastes. Just as one's body needs purification on a regular basis, so too the spiritual essence of a person needs regular cleansing.

# THOUGHT FOR TODAY:

Why is it that Hashem gives a person a spare kidney so that it is possible to donate one to save another person? (Why not, for example, a spare heart also?)

Perhaps because the lesson of the kidneys — to choose to turn away from the negative, to select the positive — is so essential in choosing friends, as our sages teach, "Either a good friend or death."

# Kidneys Are a Gift from Hashem
## (continued)

- In addition, the kidneys teach us the need to regulate ourselves, to practice self-control. We must learn to guard against excess in all matters, because too much of anything can be harmful. We must not overindulge or pamper ourselves, because our souls can only compensate for a certain amount of deviation, similar to the kidneys.

- From the kidneys' ability to correct and regulate excesses in the body, which was created and is maintained by Hashem, we realize that Hashem does the same in the world at large. He saves the afflicted and the downtrodden from their oppressors, and it is to Him that we must look for salvation. Perhaps it was these lessons that Avraham Avinu took to heart, which enabled him to reach the greatest spiritual heights.

- The Rambam (*Hilchos Dai'os* 1:7) also points out that Avraham Avinu achieved perfection in reaching and teaching the *derech Hashem*, which consists of the middle road — perfection of character which can be gained from the Divinely-inspired counsel of the kidneys.

## THOUGHT FOR TODAY:

We should think thoughts of gratitude for our kidneys when saying the Asher Yatzar blessing at intervals throughout the day. We can also say at any time: "Thank You, Hashem, for the great kidneys You have granted me in Your extreme kindness!"

# Kidneys Are a Gift from Hashem
## (continued)

- The kidneys are bean shaped, about the size of a fist. Eating kidney beans on Shabbas in the cholent can serve as a reminder for us to thank Hashem for the kidney machines that He provides us with.

- There are two of them, one on each side of the spine in the mid-back. We have to offer additional thanks to Hashem for providing two, each of which can function independently if necessary.

- Their primary function is to filter the blood and to detoxify its waste products by incorporating them into urine. They serve as the master chemists in the human body. Although they each weigh only about five ounces, they each contain within them an estimated two million filtering units which filter all the blood of the body about once every half hour.

- Blood continuously pours through them; thus they function at all times (with a slowdown during sleep). If not for them, poisons would accumulate in the body. In short, they are the laundry system of the blood and its waste disposal system.

## THOUGHT FOR TODAY:

Rav Miller suggested that when saying "Modim" each day in Shemoneh Esreh, one should select one particular concept to express gratitude for. You may find it useful to keep a daily "gratitude journal."

# Other Amazing Functions of the Kidneys

- Kidneys control potassium intake; sufficient potassium is necessary for healthy muscles, but too much potassium places undue stress upon the heart.

- They monitor the amount of sugar and salt in the body, and see that the balance of protein is just right. In addition, they produce a hormone which regulates the amount of red blood cells.

- They also adjust the amount of water in the body. Too much water and the cells would burst; too little and they would dry up.

- Scientists admit that it is beyond our present level of understanding to know all that the kidneys do!

- Hashem saw fit to provide us with plenty of kidney material to spare. Even a small percent of one of a person's kidneys would be sufficient to perform the necessary work. In addition, a damaged kidney has amazing regenerative powers.

- Most people have two kidneys, with a spare that they can donate to save someone else in need of one.

## THOUGHT FOR TODAY:

The Hebrew word for kidneys is *kelayos*, which is derived from the root word *kol*, meaning "everything." They are so essential, it is as if everything is dependent on them. Thank Hashem for yours!

# Bones Are a Gift from Hashem

- Bones are the frame of the body. Without them we would collapse like a blob of jelly. We could not walk, talk, sit, or move.

- Joints: Man cannot fully reproduce the efficiency of the ball and socket of the thigh, which allows a full range of motion, the ability to twist and turn effortlessly.

- If we would analyze the task of every bone, we would discover how its design is perfectly suited to its function. We have to thank Hashem for each bone of the body (a total of at least 248) and for their multiple functions!

- The bones at the bottom of the foot — thirty bones at our disposal — each serve a unique purpose in affording us maneuverability unequalled in machines. Picture the positioning of the foot as it climbs stairs, adjusting to each new angle, balancing the weight of the body just so, maintaining a grip so as not to slip.

# THOUGHT FOR TODAY:

Every bone in our body was positioned by Hashem with a specific plan and purpose to help save us and protect us.

# Bones Are a Gift from Hashem
## (continued)

- The bones contain the body's mineral supply. They are warehouses of calcium and phosphorus that operate twenty-four hours a day.

- In addition, the bones are factories. They manufacture millions of red blood cells that enable us to breathe, as well as a lesser amount of white blood cells which protect us from infection!

- The bones are exceptionally strong in order to protect the vulnerable parts of the body. The eyes, for example, are surrounded by a bone casing to protect them from injury, as are many other soft organs and tissues.

- "Hashem saves the helpless from those that are stronger than he" (Tehilim 35:10). Obviously, this verse is precisely the message that these bones impart: *Hashem has designed us [bones] to protect the vulnerable parts of the body!* Indeed, Hashem protects and saves people from those more powerful than they!

## THOUGHT FOR TODAY:

Just as our bones always support us, Hashem always supports us. Hashem has unlimited ways and means to do anything we need and want, and He is waiting for us to ask Him for help.

# Bones Are a Gift from Hashem
## (continued)

- The bones bear the weight of the body. Different bones are of different strengths based on where they are situated in the body and how great a part they play in weight bearing. The spinal column is light and porous so that it can accomplish its functions. Other bones are dense and super strong. In comparison, bones are stronger than a solid block of steel of the same size!

- Bones become strong as they are needed. Baby bones are soft and flexible so that they can pass through the birth canal. They maintain a certain softness throughout childhood to allow for growth and to guard against damage in scrapes and falls, and eventually they get harder toward adulthood.

- If a bone breaks, it can regenerate. A physician may put the bone back in place and plaster it in a cast to maintain the proper position, but the healing itself comes from the bone, which begins to produce overtime to replace that which is lacking. There are even "repairmen" within bones which serve to destroy the jagged edges of the break so that the bone will heal properly!

## THOUGHT FOR TODAY:

Our bones are always changing, producing, and growing, a lesson that we should be striving for spiritual growth in thanking and praising Hashem.

# Knees Are a Gift from Hashem

- Knees were intended by Hashem for bending in servitude to Him (as we do four times during the Shemonah Esrai prayer). In Nishmas it says, "Every knee will bow to You..."

- They also make it more comfortable for us to sit down (as anyone who has had the misfortune to need a cast on his leg knows).

- The feet are always ready to go without any preliminary preparations. They adapt to indoors and outdoors, and they are even amphibious. We never need to look for a place to park them, for they fold conveniently under us until the next time they are needed.

- They have a universal design that adjusts to all angles of ramps and stairs.

## THOUGHT FOR TODAY:

Feetcars are much better than streetcars! One of the purposes of knee replacement surgery is to remind us to thank Hashem for when our knees are working well. Thank Hashem for your knees!

# The Spine Is a Gift from Hashem

- The eighteen bones of the spine correspond to the eighteen (original) *brachos* (blessings) of Shemonah Esrai (*Brachos* 28b).

- We are blessed with the ability to stand upright (and the flexibility to bend the spine and the neck) so that we can bow down to serve Hashem! The text of Nishmas continues, "Every upright creature will bow to You."

- Just as bones uphold and give strength to the body, without which the body would collapse, so too Hashem has provided us with *mitzvos* which uphold our spiritual essence.

- Even if only one bone is broken, a person may suffer extensively or even be crippled (G-d forbid); so too if a person is lacking even one *mitzva*, his soul can be crippled.

## THOUGHT FOR TODAY:

The word for bone is *etzem*. The word for tree is *aitz*. The word for advice is *aitzah*. The common denominator is they are all structures for our growth!

# Hands Are a Gift from Hashem

- Hands are unique machinery — extremely sophisticated and versatile, indispensable, and constantly in use. They can be moved, maneuvered, and made to change direction. They are so complex, a combination of hinges and levers that they require thirty bones each — about one-quarter of all the bones in the body — to perform the myriad of tasks that Hashem created them for. They work effectively and swiftly, rarely tiring.

- It is estimated that a person uses his hands at least twenty-five million times throughout his life.

- We use our hands for the fine skill of writing. The coordination necessary to achieve this task is phenomenal, involving both gross and fine motor coordination of the bones, muscles, tendons, and nerves.

- Hands are efficient for many other types of precision work — surgery, watchmaking, diamond cutting, typing…

- Although they are small, hands are power packed. They can be used for a show of strength when made into a fist, and, when properly trained, as in karate, they can be lethal weapons. The strength of a person's grip is between fifty and one hundred pounds.

- These very same delicate tools also serve as more mundane utensils. They can be used as a chin rest, or a scoop, or an eating utensil. They can also serve as a repository for adornments, such as when rings or bracelets are placed upon them. These, too, were all uses that Hashem intended when He designed hands.

## THOUGHT FOR TODAY:

Each hand is called *yad*, which has a *gematria* of fourteen. Two hands together have the strength of *koach*, which has a *gematria* of twenty-eight.

# Hands Are a Gift from Hashem
## (continued)

- Hands can serve as substitutes for our other senses. They can read Braille for a sightless person, or they can serve as ears and a mouth to a deaf or mute person by enabling them to communicate through sign language. We express our feelings with a show of hands: a friendly wave, a menacing fist, or a warm handshake. Hands reinforce our feelings when we talk or clap. They can be used to motion warnings or surrender.

- Hands are masters of differentiation, thanks to millions of nerve endings concentrated in them. (There are over one thousand per square inch, and they are even more abundant in the fingertips.)

- They can pick out coins of different sizes, feel the quality of cloth, or test the texture of soil. They also detect heat, cold, and pain.

- The hands contain thirty bones apiece. With them we can write gracefully and neatly. If even one bone was missing or ailing, we would have a most difficult time doing that which is now so simple to accomplish.

- Our hands have specific *mitzva* tasks to accomplish. They are perfect for kneading dough, braiding it, and taking *challah*. They are designed just perfectly for striking a match to light Shabbas candles. They can accomplish the delicate task of writing a Torah scroll. Arms relate to the *mitzva* of *tefilin*, which we wear on the weaker arm.

## THOUGHT FOR TODAY:

> Sometimes we speak through body language. A warm handshake, hug, or pat on the back may convey, "I'm happy to see you."

# Hands Are a Gift from Hashem
## (continued)

- Fingers are miraculous inventions created by the Master Inventor. Each finger is a different size, making the hand similar to the toolbox of a master craftsman who has several of the same tools in various sizes to accomplish different jobs.

- The *sefarim* mention that each finger serves particularly as an aid to one of the five senses — one is perfectly proportioned to clean the eyes when one is weary and another is appropriate for the mouth. (Perhaps that is why babies suck their thumbs.) One serves the ears, one the nose, and one the sense of touch. They can form different size scoops and measures. We can perform calculations with them without the need for a calculator.

# THOUGHT FOR TODAY:

The Talmud (*Pesachim* 50a) says, "Fortunate are those who come to the World to Come with their Torah study in their hands." You take it with you through all the learning that you have applied and fulfilled in action.

# Hands Are a Gift from Hashem
## (continued)

- The thumb opposes the other fingers and can meet all the others. It is therefore thicker than the rest. Although, when held flat, the thumb appears shorter, when the palm is rounded, the thumb is just the right height! This serves most useful when holding objects, for the thumb functions as a balance against the other fingers. It enables us to properly grip items such as pens and eating utensils.

- Our fingertips are textured with prints, allowing for a better grip and traction. (They also allow for easier detection of criminals!) Sweat glands provide moisture for the same reason. Buttons and zippers would be difficult to maneuver without fingers.

- Our hands, of course, are the main actors in many of the *mitzvos* we do regularly:

  ◦ Giving *tzedaka* by handing over money or by writing a check for the poor

  ◦ Holding a *lulav* and *esrog* on Sukkos

  ◦ Bringing *matzah* to our mouths on Pesach

- Kneading *challah*, lighting candles
- Washing and dressing oneself in honor of Hashem
- Serving parents, etc.

## THOUGHT FOR TODAY:

"First things first" (*Avos* 5:7). The five fingers are separate to remind us: Divide things into manageable portions. Take one thing at a time, and Hashem will help you with each one.

# Feet Are a Gift from Hashem

- The foot is not designed simply like a square box, but rather it has a unique shape and curve. The shape of shoes is merely an attempt to mimic the feet which were precision made by the Creator for optimum comfort in walking and balance.

- Like our hands, each foot is composed of thirty bones, totaling approximately one quarter of the bones of the body, plus approximately one hundred ligaments and twenty muscles.

- There are additional parallels between the feet and the hands. They are both extremities of the body, and serve us in similar yet differing ways.

- There are five toes on each foot, similar to the five fingers of each hand. Both hands and feet possess thumbs that are thicker than the other digits. However, the big toe of the foot does not oppose the other toes. This is because of the basic difference between the purposes of the hands and feet.

## THOUGHT FOR TODAY:

Thank you, Hashem, for providing me with all of my needs: Even the shape of my feet suits me exactly.

# Feet Are a Gift from Hashem
## (continued)

- Hashem designed hands for the purpose of bringing things to us or away from us. Feet were designed to bring us to things or away from things. The toes are therefore not elongated for holding, but instead short for balance. They are positioned in a semicircle design to offer balance in all directions.

- Whenever the body chooses to move in a different direction, just a slight movement of the feet in that direction can accomplish the change, without the need to totally turn the foot. Similarly, the foot bends, twists, and curves just the right amount to enable us to walk up and down steps.

- The fact that the body balances itself is amazing. If the body starts falling, the foot tightens certain muscles and loosens others in order to reassert the balance. The balance differs when one is standing, walking, or running, with the body automatically compensating for all these positions.

# THOUGHT FOR TODAY:

A thank-you a day keeps trouble away.

The *Chovos Halevavos* speaks about focusing on at least one new thank-you every day so that we live with gratitude to Hashem. Scientists have studied and tested people who live with gratitude to show that they benefit in many ways: They think better, and their minds are more focused, clearer, calmer, stronger, and healthier.

# Feet Are a Gift from Hashem
## (continued)

- The Gemara (*Shabbas* 31a) tells of a person who asked Hillel why the feet of people in Africa are wider than those of people in other places. (His purpose was to tease and anger Hillel, but Hillel's answer indicates that there is a deep purpose for every phenomenon in nature.) Hillel explained that it was because those people live in muddy areas.

  ○ Rashi explains that Hashem designed their feet wider so that they would not sink in the mud that is native to their area.

  ○ Rashi then quotes an alternate interpretation. Their feet stretch because they walk barefoot in muddy areas. (Footwear would have molded and kept the foot in shape.)

- The Gemara (*Shabbas* 129a) admonishes that a person should even sell the beams of his house, if necessary, in order to purchase shoes. Without shoes, a person may get illnesses due to the environment or cut or injure his feet. It is therefore worthwhile to give up shelter, if necessary, to protect one's feet.

- The issue of footwear is so vital that our sages (*Brachos* 60b) explain the daily morning blessing "Who has provided me with all my needs" as a reference to footwear, which protect the feet.

## THOUGHT FOR TODAY:

There is a saying, "If the shoe fits, wear it." We should add, also *enjoy* it with the realization that Hashem saw to it that it was made in your size and that you found your way to that store to get what you need.

# Feet Are a Gift from Hashem
## (continued)

- In addition to balancing the body, the feet also support the weight of the body.

- Walking is even more complex than balancing and standing. The body moves in an intricate rhythm. It is estimated that the average person walks over one hundred thousand miles in his lifetime.

- The skin of the sole of the foot is up to ten times thicker than elsewhere in the body, for protection and padding — a form of built-in shoes. In addition, the foot protects itself against bruises and pressure by responding to stress and developing corns and callouses, which serve to protect the feet from injury.

- The feet contribute to our overall good health by providing us with exercise.

- There are also many incidental uses for which we must not neglect to thank Hashem, such as kicking a door open when necessary, in which case the foot serves as an extra hand;

peddling a bicycle for fun, exercise, and transportation; using feet to drive a car; or running a foot pedal on a sewing machine or other equipment.

# THOUGHT FOR TODAY:

Are you happy that you can stand on your own feet? Not everyone can do so. It is a great gift from Hashem which we need to acknowledge daily and utilize it for joy! "Who is wealthy? One who rejoices with his portions!" (Avos 4:1).

# Feet Are a Gift from Hashem
## (continued)

- We recognize the benefits of our "Cadillac" legs in providing us with twenty-four-hour, ever-ready transportation.

- When we arrive at our destination, there is no need to look for a parking space. Our legs tuck conveniently under us should we desire to sit. If we do not find a comfortable spot to sit, or prefer to stand, our feet lock into place to allow us to maintain that position.

- All these uses and many more are obvious uses of our feet, and were intended in the original design of the foot by Hashem. We make a special *brachah* every morning to thank Hashem for these benefits, "Who prepares the steps of man" (*Brachos* 60b).

## THOUGHT FOR TODAY:

Each and every step you take is a gift from Hashem. Being able to get up and walk around is a unique blessing you should be excited about. Appreciate walking without pain.

# The Mouth Is a Gift from Hashem

- The mouth is a multifaceted instrument that serves us in many ways. It is a utensil that is capable of taking, processing, and transporting food toward the food pipe. Drinking constitutes a different art than eating. The mouth not only chews and bites, but the lips also suck liquids and the cheeks are designed appropriately to contain liquids and to propel them toward the food pipe.

- The mouth is a versatile mouthpiece and musical instrument, similar to a pipe organ, and its vocal cords are similar to violin strings. It can produce all kinds of sounds: speaking, singing, shouting, humming. It has its own amplifying system, which can be raised or lowered.

- When one's nose is stuffed, he can compensate by breathing through the mouth. The air will still reach his lungs and keep him alive.

- Coughing is in itself a miracle. Scientists have noted that coughing is an incredible protective mechanism. If something gets lodged in the throat, the body traps air and expels it in a forceful blast that can reach up to two hundred miles per hour.

## THOUGHT FOR TODAY:

Before every Shemoneh Esrai, we ask Hashem to "please *open our lips* and enable our mouths to relate Your praise" (Tehilim 51:17). Opening our lips is in itself a miracle. Hashem gives us the energy to move and open them.

# The Mouth Is a Gift from Hashem
## (continued)

- The epiglottis closes whenever we swallow to protect against food entry into the trachea. This remarkable double system may be compared to two sets of train tracks that are intertwined at points and must be synchronized to avoid collisions. Food follows the path to the esophagus, while air follows the same path to the lungs. The tongue serves as a conveyor belt to deliver food to the proper channel. However, one who is attempting to talk while chewing food may disrupt this mechanism, allowing food to lodge in the windpipe and causing choking.

- It is not a coincidence that a person can open his mouth wide. The purpose is not merely so that he can fill it with a huge sandwich or a large bite of apple. We are rather encouraged to eat in small bites in order to control our passions, and to demonstrate that we eat in order to have strength to serve Hashem. It is when one prays to Hashem that he is encouraged to open his mouth wide, i.e., to ask for all that he desires, for this indicates that he realizes that Hashem is the all-powerful Source of everything (*Brachos* 50a).

- It is a tremendous pleasure to let loose in song. Song livens the spirit and makes life easier and more enjoyable.

## THOUGHT FOR TODAY:

What an amazing miracle that the same mouth that eats can also speak!

The ear or eyes are not able to eat. Why did Hashem choose the mouth for these dual functions? One lesson is to remind us that just as we need kosher food to fuel our systems, so too we may only speak kosher words as we communicate with others to fuel our interactions with the world.

# Ears Are a Gift from Hashem

- The ears protrude on both sides of the head. The part we see, the outer ear, is not the real ear, but rather a sound-gathering machine which accumulates sounds for us to hear.

- Ears are equipped with whorls and hollows to catch and gather sound waves. There are four thousand arches, one within the other, with the most precise, fine measurement.

- They are perched strategically on both sides of the head like earphones. (We can also tell which side the sounds are from.)

- The ears are composed of thin and resilient cartilage so that they fold neatly out of the way when the head is placed on a pillow, without the slightest discomfort. (Had they been of a stiffer material, they might crack or cause discomfort.)

## THOUGHT FOR TODAY:

Your power of listening is one means of doing kindness to others. Learn to listen to others. Both what they say and what they leave unsaid provide clues to what they need: perhaps your help, your *tzedaka*, or just your listening ear.

# Ears Are a Gift from Hashem
## (continued)

- The outer ear serves as a hanger for glasses and hats, and also as an ideal spot for wearing earrings for those who desire to do so. These are intentional benefits in their design by the Creator, and for these too we must be grateful.

- There is a one-inch canal between the inner ear and outer ear that is twisted rather than straight. This serves to protect the delicate, inner components of the ear and to warm the air before it enters so that it will not be abrasive. In addition, the canal is lined with hairs which also protect the inner mechanisms.

- The ears lubricate themselves with an ear wax. The ear contains about four thousand wax glands which serve as a sticky fly-paper trap to help guard against infection and to keep out insects and dust.

# THOUGHT FOR TODAY:

Why does Hashem give us two ears and two eyes but only one mouth?

The Vilna Gaon, Mishlai 11:2, explains:

- Two eyes — to study the Written Torah.
- Two ears — to listen to the Oral Law.
- Only one mouth — not to speak so much.

# Ears Are a Gift from Hashem
## (continued)

- The inner ear contains the eardrum, upon which sound waves strike. These drums are so sensitive that they can even detect a whisper. The inner ear contains enough electrical circuits to provide telephone service for an entire city!

- The auditory nerve is about the size of the lead in a pencil, yet it is so complex that it contains about thirty thousand circuits. It amplifies that which we hear twenty-two times.

- Another function of the ears is to regulate our balance. Just as tightrope walkers have a balancing pole to allow them to walk on thin wire, so our ears serve as balancing poles, on automatic pilot. If the body tips a bit to one side, the ears register the change and send messages to the brain to correct the deficiency. This is why the ears are called in Hebrew *oznayim* — from the word *moznayim*, which refers to balance scales.

# THOUGHT FOR TODAY:

Thank Hashem for the outer frame of the ears, which are soft and pliable so that they don't crack when we turn our heads at night in bed.

# Eyes Are a Gift from Hashem

- The eye is safely recessed in a protruding bone frame, which protects it from blows.

- It is furnished with a lid, which rolls down automatically whenever an object approaches, and which rolls up conveniently out of sight when not in use. (Imagine a windshield wiper that turns on automatically when it starts to rain.)

- The eyebrows intercept perspiration, and the eyelashes help keep out foreign matter.

- The eye is continuously being bathed in a soothing and antiseptic fluid, supplied by the wells of the tear ducts.

- The eye is self-adjusting for light intensity and self-focusing to adjust for distance. It takes color pictures and rotates to focus on all sides.

# THOUGHT FOR TODAY:

The word *aino*, "his eye," has a *gematria* of 136, which is the same as *mamon* (money) — 136. This teaches us that a person's perception is influenced by various factors, such as monetary bribes or incentives. Thus we are taught that a person should always study Torah and perform *mitzvos* even for ulterior motives, so that eventually it will develop into *lishma*, for the sake of serving Hashem.

# Eyes Are a Gift from Hashem
## (continued)

- The eye functions as an information-gathering machine that immediately reports its findings to the brain, which interprets and makes use of the information.

- The eye is amazingly complex and concentrated with tens of millions of electrical connections.

- It has the ability to process one million messages simultaneously. The sights that we see are extremely meaningful, not lifeless like the pictures of a camera. All messages that are received are analyzed, stored on file, and integrated.

- Scientists estimate that the eyes generally gather approximately 80 percent of all the knowledge that a person absorbs in his lifetime.

# THOUGHT FOR TODAY:

The first of three character traits that enable us to become disciples of Avraham Avinu is to develop a good eye. This is explained to include to be satisfied with what one has and not to desire what belongs to others. This is based on "seeing" the whole world with the perspective that Hashem is the Creator and Provider, and everything He does is for the best.

Some see a cup half empty; some see it half full. We should see it overflowing with Hashem's blessings.

# Eyes Are a Gift from Hashem
## (continued)

- The retina of the eye contains 137 million light-sensitive receptor cells — 130 million shaped like rods, which detect black-and-white vision, and 7 million shaped like cones for color vision. This is an additional gift Hashem bestows upon most people — the gift of color vision!

- The muscles of the eye are the strongest of the entire body. They move about one hundred thousand times a day, serving the person in many ways.

- Hashem gave us two eyes to provide the perception of depth and distance. In addition, each eye has an assistant in order to provide it with a chance to rest. One eye may work while the other rests.

- The eyes have their own extraordinary cleansing mechanism. There are windshield wipers (eyelids) to keep out the dust and rain, and tears to remove any particles that may enter the eye.

# THOUGHT FOR TODAY:

"One who has a good attitude is always at a party" (Mishlai 15:15).

Some people spend time and effort learning how to appreciate so-called art. The Torah teaches us to spend time and effort on the art of appreciation! We need to learn to see the good in every person and in everything.

# Eating Is a Gift from Hashem

- The eyes first scan the food to see whether its color indicates ripeness or deterioration.

- The nose tests the odor of the food to detect its desirability for entry. This function is one of the reasons for the shape and position of the nose — situated as a sentry above the mouth.

- The lips serve as a sucking disk and they prevent liquids from spilling out. The cheeks expand and contract in proportion to the amount of food in the mouth.

- The tongue and the elastic cheeks manipulate the morsel toward the rear of the mouth.

- The saliva assists by softening the food and beginning the digestive process. It also lubricates the process of chewing and swallowing.

- The tongue darts back and forth, testing the food for admission to the inner body and feeling out bits of bone and other inedible matter which would be injurious if swallowed.

# THOUGHT FOR TODAY:

When Tosfos (*Brachos* 37a) searches for an example to illustrate that Hashem designed this world for us to enjoy pleasure, it explains that Hashem created apples for us to eat and enjoy!

# The Heart Is a Gift from Hashem

- The heart is a reddish-brown colored organ that weighs about twelve ounces. It is approximately six inches long and four inches wide and hangs suspended from ligaments in the center of the chest. (You do not have to keep recharging it or plugging it in, or even flip an on-and-off switch!)

- Primarily, the heart serves as a hard-working pump — in fact, it actually consists of two pumps. It has two sections, each containing two compartments, the right side and the left side, and each has a specific pumping activity to accomplish. The left side draws deoxygenated, waste-laden blood from the body to the lungs to be refreshed. The right side is responsible for returning the rejuvenated blood to the entire body about once every thirty seconds.

- This activity occurs nonstop, throughout the day and night for 70 to 120 years. Every day the heart pumps blood through approximately sixty thousand miles of blood vessels. In a lifetime, it moves about five hundred thousand tons of blood.

- The heart is considered to be the strongest and hardest working of all the muscles in constant use within the body. It has its own self-generator, an automatic, internal ignition system. It needs no cranking, starting, or pilot light. It has its own self-nourishment system, the coronary arteries. These require about one-twentieth of the entire blood supply, which the heart also supplies.

- In most cases the heart functions uncomplainingly and almost noiselessly. It increases its pace when we increase ours and adjusts to our needs when we slow down.

## THOUGHT FOR TODAY:

*The first letter of the Torah is a bais, and the last letter is a lamed, which serves to remind us that our laiv (heart) is essential in applying ourselves to and fulfilling Hashem's Torah.*

# Body Protection Is a Gift from Hashem

- The blood contains a coagulating agent which is inactive until the skin is cut and the blood comes into contact with the air. It then clots the wound to prevent excessive blood loss.

- The fingers are the tools which produce all of one's physical achievements, and they also have an additional, even greater function by serving in the performance of certain *mitzvos*, and in their usefulness (as ear plugs) to close the ears against hearing undesirable words (*Kesubos* 5b).

- The stomach's digestive acids break down the toughest of foods, but they do not digest the stomach lining itself.

- The body produces antibodies whereby a disease leaves over a substance which immunizes the body against a second onslaught.

## THOUGHT FOR TODAY:

Imagine using and moving only your small finger to fulfill all your needs. In contrast, study and consider how abundant are the great resources Hashem supplies you. Appreciate them and thank Hashem.

# Body Protection Is a Gift from Hashem (continued)

- The body's energy supply is self-regulating; when it runs low in fuel, the sensation of hunger takes over. When the water supply runs low, the sensation of thirst prompts us to drink water.

- If not for these systems, a person may deplete his stock and simply stop short in the street, like an automobile which runs out of gas on the road. As soon as one has restored his fuel supply, he loses his urgent desire to eat.

- In combat or flight, additional sugar is injected into the bloodstream to supply added energy, and a clotting agent enters the blood to prepare to stop up possible wounds.

- Hashem designed the body with built-in protection systems. "Who is wise? One who foresees what might develop" (*Tamid* 32a).

# THOUGHT FOR TODAY:

Just as you are careful to keep your car full of fuel, enough to last you for your upcoming trip, so too we should fuel our thoughts daily with "Thank You, Hashem" thoughts for the gifts we receive daily. To generate love of Hashem, we need the right fuel in daily dosages.

# Teeth Are a Gift from Hashem

- The front teeth are all sharp edged to cut off pieces of food into convenient-sized pieces for chewing. The multi-surfaced back teeth grind the food.

- The teeth are cloaked with a marvelously hard, smooth enamel substance which render them suitable for chewing all kinds of food. The jaws have a surprisingly powerful leverage which enables them to exert great pressure in biting and chewing.

- Besides functioning as an eating tool, teeth serve also for the function of speech and as a framework for the lips and cheeks.

- The teeth of the upper jaw overlap the corresponding teeth in the lower jaw in order to prevent the cheeks from getting bitten each time the jaws close.

- The white color of the teeth serves to brighten people's lives when others show the white of their teeth in a smile! (*Kesubos* 111b)

# THOUGHT FOR TODAY:

Rabbi Miller, *zt"l*, would ask his dentist: Have you ever seen a person whose front teeth were in the rear of his mouth and whose molars were in the front? Never! Hashem designed it this way purposefully: the front teeth bite the food into small pieces so that they can be chewed by the molars in the rear.

# Teeth Are a Gift from Hashem
## (continued)

- The teeth begin the eating process. Hashem gave a person a mouth full of silverware — sharp front teeth which serve as knives to cut food, molars in the back to grind, and four pointed teeth to tear food when necessary. It is important to consider the ingenious engineering of our teeth and to thank the Master Engineer for them. Although one could eat without teeth, much of the convenience and enjoyment would be lost. The food would have to be pulverized, and the pleasure of chewing would be lost.

- Teeth serve as the frame for the mouth. If not for teeth, the mouth would collapse.

- Babies' mouths are designed for nursing so that they can benefit from the nourishment most suited to them. They are therefore born without teeth. At approximately six months of age, when they begin to need other foods, the teeth start to grow out and the shape of the mouth adapts to better allow for chewing. As the jaw begins to grow to adult size, the baby teeth fall out in order to allow for larger teeth to grow in more suited to an adult. But only one tooth falls out at a time, so that the child can continue to chew food in the interim! (*Chovos Halevavos, Bechina* 5)

- Teeth assist in the speaking process.

## THOUGHT FOR TODAY:

Why did Hashem desire that children experience teething pain when their teeth develop? *Chovos Halevavos* explains it is to train people to recognize that this world has challenges and discomforts, and we need Hashem's help to overcome and succeed.

# Hips Are a Gift from Hashem

- The hip is a perfectly designed ball-and-socket joint that can rotate millions of times without needing oiling or servicing and can carry up to fifteen times its normal load. It is the largest, most stable body joint.

- The ball and socket are smoothly contoured and fit snugly together. Each is lined with a layer of rubbery cartilage that acts as an elastic cushion which allows the ball to rotate smoothly in the socket.

- The ball and socket are further joined together by sheets and strands of muscles and ligaments. The joint is completely enclosed in a tough capsule of ligament tissue lined with a membrane that secretes a slippery fluid to lubricate the joint.

# THOUGHT FOR TODAY:

When Yaakov Avinu was cured from his limp (Beraishis 32:33), the Torah describes how the sun helped cure him. Then the Torah explains that he was *shalaim* (complete). He was physically well, financially complete, and spiritually whole (*Rashi*, Beraishis 33:18).

We need to pray for these three gifts daily and to thank Hashem for His ongoing benefits in each of these areas.

# The Brain Is a Gift from Hashem

- The brain consists of about three pounds of grey and white tissues, which function as an amazing computer with extraordinary capacities. No computer comes near to duplicating its myriad functions. It is estimated to be capable of storing fifteen trillion separate pieces of information, and it can simultaneously receive and transmit as many messages as one thousand large switchboards, of the type needed for a city as densely populated as New York.

- The brain contains a staggering number of components: about thirty billion nerve cells that are all interconnected — some as many as sixty thousand times — all in the compact size of the human skull! To perform all these functions, the brain uses about 20 percent of the body's blood supply and about 25 percent of its oxygen supply.

- The brain never sleeps. It is constantly busy, evaluating, processing, and responding to information, even when we are asleep.

# THOUGHT FOR TODAY:

"You grant to a person intelligence and You teach us understanding" (Shemonah Esrai).

This is the greatest and the most fundamental of all gifts: a computer brain that runs all our body processes.

# The Brain Is a Gift from Hashem
## (continued)

- The brain is diverse. It can select and concentrate on one thought even while it is working on several others. It is known that many sages were able to accomplish more than one task at the same time. Rav Chaim Ozer was known to be able to write two different *teshuvos* — one with each hand — while conversing on a third topic with a visitor!

- The brain serves as a built-in alarm system. It recognizes danger signals and allows one to react to them either to avoid the danger altogether or to minimize its results. It then allows one to experience pain, both in order to take proper healing steps and also to record the experience in our memory so that we will prevent similar situations in the future.

- The brain serves as housekeeper for the entire body. It performs thousands of chores that we don't even think about, such as breathing, digestion, etc....

## THOUGHT FOR TODAY:

When we summarize the purpose of life in Tehilim 90, we say, "Please teach us to count our days properly so that we develop a heart of wisdom." Learn to count your days and to make your days count!

# The Brain Is a Gift from Hashem
## (continued)

- The brain never forgets completely. It is a fact that everything that a person saw or did in his entire lifetime is recorded somewhere in his brain. Every activity, no matter how trivial, is stored and registered in the mind.

- Yet, the brain does forget. The *Chovos Halevavos* (*Bechina* 5) teaches that if not for forgetting, if one would never be relieved of sorrow, and no joy could expel it from his mind, and nothing would bring him pleasure when he remembers the misfortunes in this world. He would remain constantly depressed.

- The brain has its own backup system. Each item is stored in the brain in various places and forms, and from various perspectives, so that although the brain does not regenerate or repair itself, it can replace the activities of the damaged areas.

## THOUGHT FOR TODAY:

Hashem, who invented our brain, is in complete control of it. He gives us free will and provides guidelines (Torah and *mitzvos*) how to use it. We say this verse daily: "There are many thoughts in a person and the plans of Hashem will come to fruition" (Mishlai 19:21).

# Walking Is a Gift from Hashem

- The thigh swings forward in effortless motion on smoothly functioning joints, bathed in a friction-preventing liquid.

- The knee bends and straightens again and again, without any sensation of chafing or scraping.

- The ankle joints and the complex arch bones flex and relax in easy motion. The average person takes 19,000 steps a day, enough to cover eight miles. Each step should prompt us to be grateful to the Creator.

- The shape of the bottom of both feet make it easy to maintain one's balance.

- A person's two feet are the same length from birth and they continuously grow at the same rate during their time of growth.

## THOUGHT FOR TODAY:

*What is it that you really want? Hashem has created and designed us so that if you desire a certain outcome and walk in that direction, Hashem will get us there: "On the path one is determined to go, Hashem will lead him" (Makos 10b).*

# The Liver Is a Gift from Hashem

- The liver is an organ weighing approximately three pounds (the largest of the body), protected by the ribs and located in the upper right of the abdomen. Its functions are so complex that scientists estimate that it performs over five hundred different jobs.

- To duplicate even a few of the liver's simplest functions, we would need large factories with acres of machinery. The more complex functions cannot yet be duplicated by man.

- It provides fuel for the muscles of the body, which are necessary for all our activities.

- It produces vitamin A, which is essential for healthy vision and for the ability to overcome night blindness.

- It produces over one thousand different enzymes that process all types of materials!

- The miracle of blood clotting depends on the liver's production of vitamin K. What a marvelous ability! (Vitamin K is produced in the body from the eighth day after birth — just in time for the *bris*.)

## THOUGHT FOR TODAY:

Hashem has infinite ways of making things happen. We have to keep saying, "How great are Your creations, Hashem, how deep are Your thoughts" (Tehilim 92:6).

# The Liver Is a Gift from Hashem
## (continued)

- The liver produces antibodies which protect us from outside invaders that cause disease.

- It changes potentially deadly amino acids into proteins, the building blocks of our muscles and genetic materials. It changes surplus acid into urea, which is then passed to the kidneys where it can be excreted safely. It detoxifies chemicals and poisons, which the body ingests.

- The liver is a thrifty housekeeper. It stores surpluses of materials that the body can use but has too much of at present. For example, it salvages products from red blood cells as they are destroyed, to be reused in fresh cells.

# THOUGHT FOR TODAY:

*There is a powerful lesson here in that things can be changed! We can change and transform our thoughts and ways to serve Hashem. When we choose to do what is right, Hashem helps us succeed.*

# The Liver Is a Gift from Hashem
## (continued)

- The liver aids digestion by secreting bile, about one quart daily, which is then stored in the gall bladder and released at meal times in order to digest fat into small globules and to help wash away fat deposits.

- If the liver is not functioning properly, Hashem provides a color indicator — jaundice — to alert us to the fact that something is wrong.

- The liver has a tremendous capacity to regenerate itself from certain types of damage. If even 85 percent of it is destroyed, the remainder can continue to function and actually repair itself within a few weeks.

- In *lashon hakodesh*, the liver is called *kavaid* (heavy), because it is the heaviest and busiest organ.

## THOUGHT FOR TODAY:

Hashem is constantly guiding and directing us. One message here is that Hashem tells us, "I am doing most of the heavy work for you. I need you to keep on making some decisions, such as to choose to eat healthy foods, but I will process them for you and make your body work!"

# Skin Is a Gift from Hashem

- Every square inch of skin contains approximately:

    - 4 million cells
    - 5 yards of nerves
    - 4 feet of blood vessels
    - 120 sweat glands
    - 20 oil glands
    - 30 nerve endings

- The skin manufactures vitamin D in the presence of sunlight.

- It assists in regulating the body's blood pressure by reacting to the heat and environmental conditions.

- The skin serves to waterproof the body. It keeps water out of the body when one is immersed in a tub or a pool, and it keeps water in so that a person will not dehydrate.

- It contains a complex nervous system. All throughout the skin there are nerve endings which perceive pain, heat, and cold, and also provide the sense of touch.

# THOUGHT FOR TODAY:

The skin does more for the body than a bulletproof vest. When we thank Hashem in the first *brachah* of Shemoneh Esrai for "shielding Avraham" (*magain Avraham*), this message is included: Thank you, Hashem, for the skin You provided Avraham with, and for the skin You give us!

# Skin Is a Gift from Hashem
## (continued)

- The skin is the frontier of the body. It serves as a shield to protect the body from the environment, like a suit of armor. The invasion of bacteria is arrested by the skin, unless there is a break in its surface.

- When a break does occur in the skin, it has the remarkable ability to regenerate itself. The skin will actually reunite itself. We must appreciate the incredible phenomenon of such a miracle! Imagine a garment which, if it tears, would mend itself within a week or two. How much would such a garment be worth? Scientists consider this engineering feat to be even more complicated than the erection of a huge skyscraper.

- The skin renews itself on a regular basis. In about a month, a human being grows a new outer skin, although this is not noticeable because it develops gradually. (Imagine a garment that could constantly replenish its outer layer.)

- The skin serves as an insulator to conserve body heat. It also provides air-conditioning, which is extremely important, especially during the summertime. The system, consisting of about two million sweat glands all over the body and about six miles of ducts, is very complex. By causing the body to manufacture sweat which evaporates from the surface of the skin, the body is cooled.

## THOUGHT FOR TODAY:

A *metzora* may be punished measure for measure with a severe skin disease because he was not careful to avoid *lashon hara*, which hurts people's feelings. Be sensitive to people's feelings. Never say words that may embarrass, insult, or offend anyone.

# Skin Is a Gift from Hashem
## (continued)

- The skin serves as a shock absorber. Areas that receive the most wear produce even extra protection by forming callouses. Different parts of the body have different types of skin, harder and softer, and even differing amounts of hair (which the skin also produces), based on the need of protection in that specific area. The skin is also remarkably elastic in order to allow for the many positions and flexing of the body and limbs.

- The skin is an indicator of the body's general state of health. It can convey health or pallor, youth or age. (This is similar to the peel of a fruit, which is used to judge its ripeness and suitability for eating.) In general, the skin serves as a heavenly bestowed shield that surrounds us with protection.

- Trembling is an emotional reaction that is connected to the skin. Extreme fear causes the blood vessels to shut down and the person experiences trembling. (Shivering stimulates blood circulation to warm and protect the body in times of distress.)

# THOUGHT FOR TODAY:

The skin serves as a fence to protect the body from much harm. It also serves as a model — develop a thick skin! Learn to ignore insults as if it is blocked by your skin. The Talmud (*Sanhedrin* 7a) teaches, "How fortunate is one who hears and ignores; he will be saved from one hundred troubles."

# SHAAR III
# THE WORLD IS A GIFT FROM HASHEM

Thank you, Hashem, for billions of gifts!

# Flowers Are Gifts from Hashem

- The main purpose of flowers, fruits, and all other things in the wide, wonderful universe is to make us aware of the Creator.

- Blowing on a seed ball and viewing the miraculous spectacle of these G-d-made floating parachutes is the ultimate purpose of the flower.

- The flower is therefore *very good* in all of its aspects. The most meaningful of its benefits is that it demonstrates and points to its Creator. It is as if each flower were imprinted with a label, "By Hashem."

## THOUGHT FOR TODAY:

> Rabbi Miller, zt"l, explained when you walk by a flower it is like seeing a burning bush. We are obligated to pause and think, "Look at this miracle. What is Hashem's message to me with this unique phenomena?"

# Flowers Are Gifts from Hashem
## (continued)

- Flowers are wondrously complex and minute laboratories of photosynthesis and numerous other intricate processes.

- The petals are all in a symmetrical design. The stem is an architectural wonder designed with osmosis elevators that raise water and dissolved materials from the earth to distribute them to the leaves and flowers. (It is miraculous that the sucking action of the roots raise only those materials which the plant needs out of the earth.)

- Every flower of every healthy plant is perfectly shaped, and the outline and design of every plant has individual character, beauty lines, and grace. Its coloring is also delightfully distributed and so natural!

# THOUGHT FOR TODAY:

Hashem created the world for us to enjoy and be happy. As the *Mesilas Yesharim* teaches, "A person was created only for having joy with Hashem." We learn lessons from flowers such as be smiley, cheerful, relaxed, and friendly. Learn to enjoy the beauty of flowers!

# Flowers Are Gifts from Hashem
(continued)

- Each stigma is either sticky or fuzzy so that it traps pollen grains that touch it. The pollen then descends to produce more seeds. The stigmas face in all directions in the form of a maze so as to catch as many grains of pollen as possible.

- The showy petals signal the presence of food and serve as convenient landing platforms. Patterns of lines and spots, called honey guides, lead insect visitors to the stores of nectar or pollen. Scent is another powerful attractant, especially on night-blooming species that would otherwise be difficult to find.

- Flowers present a beautiful display of color, variation, and fragrance. Wonders upon wonders! "Open up your eyes on high, and see Who created these" (Yeshaya 40:26). Upon viewing these sights we should acquire an inkling of the greatness of He Who created them.

## THOUGHT FOR TODAY:

Why are there so many different colors and shapes? The Talmud (*Rosh Hashana*) says this stirs us to recognize the Creator Who made them all. Each style catches our eye to be inspired to exclaim: Wow! Who is the unique artist of this masterpiece?

# The Sun Is a Gift from Hashem

- The sun provides light to see by and to enjoy, and marks the days and the seasons. The sun does not rise suddenly, but rather gradually, to prevent injury to the eyes.

- It provides lifesaving warmth and health-giving vitamin D by means of its rays.

- It raises by evaporation the world's rain supply and is essential to the process of photosynthesis whereby all vegetation and food exists.

- If you could invent a light bulb that generates heat and light and also fills your refrigerator with food, you would become very wealthy. The sun does all this and more.

## THOUGHT FOR TODAY:

The sun is a metaphor for the Torah, which is called light — "*Torah Or.*" You can be outside and see light all around, but it is still dark if you don't study Torah to see the true light of Hashem.

# The Sun Is a Gift from Hashem
## (continued)

- The sun supplies the light of the moon (which serves as a useful night lamp; it is not bright enough to hinder sleep).

- The sun teaches us about Hashem's glory: "The heavens declare the glory of G-d" (Tehilim 19:2). By viewing the luminaries, we see a little of His might. When a ruler demanded to see the god of the Jews, Rabbi Yehoshua ben Chanania told him to first look at the sun. When he claimed that he was unable to do so, the sage said, "If you are unable to look at one of the servants that stands before G-d, how can you expect to look at G-d Himself?" (*Chulin* 60a)

- The longest *brachah* in the *siddur* is for creating the light of the sun, which we say each morning after Barchu. It is so important because the sun is the power source that powers everything in life.

# THOUGHT FOR TODAY:

Solar power keeps us alive. You can become happy right now by thinking of the glorious sun Hashem created for each one of us. "Who is wealthy? One who rejoices with his great portions" (*Avos* 4:1).

# Water Is a Gift from Hashem

- When necessary, water becomes lighter than air and rises in the form of water vapor to form clouds.
- Two gases, hydrogen and oxygen, neither of which can quench thirst separately, are combined into a clear, sparkling, and life-giving liquid.
- It is the vehicle of digestion, of blood circulation, of the numerous body secretions, and of the process of expulsion of waste materials. It brings nutrients to every organ and to every cell, and it carries away the wastes at the same time.
- It is the lubricating agent in the mucous membranes, in the joints, in the eyes, and between all moving parts, and it is the major part of our body weight. It cools the body through perspiration.

## THOUGHT FOR TODAY:

When you are thirsty and take a drink of water, you first recite the blessing "*Shehakol niyeh bidvaro*" (that everything was created by His word). Water is so precious that it is called "everything"!

# Rain Is a Gift from Hashem

- Rain enables the earth to produce (directly and also indirectly) good things to eat: bread, cake, meat, fish, and fruits such as apples, pears, watermelons, strawberries, tomatoes, carrots, peppers, onions, lettuce…

- Rain provides water, wine, and other beverages to drink. It provides water for bathing and for washing clothes, plus water for rivers and lakes, for green fields and forests, and for your lawn.

- "A day of rain is greater than the day of the Giving of the Torah" (*Taanis* 7a). Without rain, we would not be able to exist, and the Torah would not be maintained. Entire future *yeshivos* are therefore descending now from the rain clouds.

- The rain falls at certain times and in the proper dosages. The water does not pour down in heavy masses but in small drops, which do not cause injury.

- If a supermarket would deliver to your home a truck full of free groceries, would you grumble that your kitchen was being cluttered up with boxes and crates of gift merchandise?

# THOUGHT FOR TODAY:

Some people want to win a "lottery." You just did, if you have:

- ° Legs to walk with
- ° Oxygen to breathe
- ° A tongue for speaking and eating
- ° Toes to walk and balance with
- ° energy for good health and excitement
- ° rain and running water
- ° yearning for growth and closeness to Hashem

# Thorns Are Gifts from Hashem

- In order to protect the lovely rose from predation by man or beast, Hashem has provided the rosebush with weapons: dagger-like thorns. Although the bark of the bush is of a plain, rough material, the thorns are tough, smooth, and sharp to deter those who may try to uproot the bush.

- Why did Hashem invent thorns for this purpose? Does the Creator desire to spoil all the fun? The thorns are only on the stems, not on the flowers themselves. Obviously, they serve to protect the bush from being uprooted, so that there will be flowers growing next week and next year, too. We must therefore rejoice and thank Hashem for the thorns, too, since they preserve the beauty of the rose!

- Cactus spines deter animals from making a meal of the cactus's fleshy stem. Why did Hashem create these in a different form from the rose's thorns? Why are the cactus's spines composed of many points that are set out in clusters and rows? These spines serve as additional surface areas to help cool the body and to also trap an insulating layer of air close to the cactus. They also reduce evaporation by breaking up drying breezes and air currents. The spines act as collectors of rain and dewdrops and gently drip the water to the soil at the foot of the cactus and the roots below.

## THOUGHT FOR TODAY:

*Some people ask, "Why do roses have thorns?"*
*Others remark, "Look, thorns have roses!"*

# The Venus Flytrap Is a Gift from Hashem

- The venus flytrap plant has flytraps at its tip. Each trap is hinged down the middle, and stays open until it closes on its prey.

- The center of the trap contains three trigger hairs, which cause it to shut. When an insect touches two out of the three hairs, or the same hair twice, the leaf locks closed over the insect and remains shut until it digests its victim.

- The center of the leaf is attractively colored to serve as bait for the insect.

## THOUGHT FOR TODAY:

Hashem helps us learn how to think. He created everything with a unique plan and purpose so that we recognize His infinite wisdom and kindness. As we say in the Shabbas prayers, "*Gadlo v'tuvo malai olam*—His greatness and goodness fills the world."

# Clothing Is a Gift from Hashem

- Hashem has prepared cotton, wool, and other materials which can be spun and woven into valuable and dignified articles of clothing. Some garments are of light and soft material, pleasant to the skin; others are of heavy material to keep the body warm.

- Buttons and buttonholes are excellent contrivances to fasten together the garments; the buttons are waterproof and the buttonholes are rimmed to prevent tearing. (Hashem has not only prepared the materials necessary for these inventions, but He also provides people with the inventive ideas.)

- The linings in some garments make them more comfortable. Pockets are handy containers for objects of use.

- The garments are dyed with pleasing colors.

- Particular garments such as socks are soft and comfortable and made to fit the shape of the foot.

- Each garment should be viewed as a manifold kindliness. By studying each one individually, a person will be able to fully appreciate the thanks we express daily in the blessing for clothing.

## THOUGHT FOR TODAY:

Hashem provides us with clothing to cover our body to help us realize that we are not the physical. We are the soul, the *neshama* within the body.

# Shoes Are a Gift from Hashem

- They are made of durable and comfortable leather which are also dyed and polished.

- They are lined for comfort. The rubber heels make walking comfortable. The hard soles protect the feet.

- Shoes can be tightened with laces or Velcro to keep them in place. They can be loosened to make them easier to put on and take off. Shoelaces are tipped with plastic for convenience.

## THOUGHT FOR TODAY:

As we walk through the day and through life, our shoes stay with us. They come attached wherever we go. So too we make choices to study Torah and do mitzvos and they become part of us. Thinking, speaking, and acting with positive, pure thoughts bring us closer to Hashem. When we walk with Him, He will be there for us.

# Wind Is a Gift from Hashem

- The wind plants many seeds, causing countless grasses and trees to grow. It also prunes the dead branches off trees.

- The winds transport the clouds inland to where rain is needed. Wind purifies the atmosphere by clearing away air pollution and by air-conditioning the surroundings. Wind movement of air regulates the climate.

- The winds are His messengers (Tehilim 104:4) that sweep and sprinkle, to clean the face of the earth (*Chulin* 60a). They cool us like a fan on a hot day.

## THOUGHT FOR TODAY:

Wind power is amazing, yet you can push your hand right through it. There is a powerful lesson here: Hashem is showing us that a batch of air can produce energy to create food and empower life. Wind also teaches us that our fleeting thoughts (which may resemble air) can change our lives and transform the world.

# Eggs Are Gifts from Hashem

- An egg is a package of tasty and nourishing protein and vitamin A. It is easily digestible, requires little preparation, and can be eaten quickly.

- The abundance of eggs causes them to be relatively inexpensive.

- Birds' eggs are mottled, to escape detection, whereas hens' eggs are not mottled, in order to be conspicuous to the farmer, who can use them for human consumption.

- Chickens produce eggs in abundance so that there is always an adequate supply for human sustenance.

- They are produced in a handy container just the right size for a single serving.

- Eggs can be prepared in many ways: soft-boiled, hard-boiled, scrambled, or other ways. They are very useful in the preparation of many pastries and food dishes.

## THOUGHT FOR TODAY:

The incredible egg is an example of a small-sized product that is so useful and beneficial. It serves as a reminder that a righteous person should "say less and do a lot" (*Avos* 1:15).

# Fruits Are Gifts from Hashem

- Unripe fruits are green to make them unnoticeable amongst the leaves and unattractive to the eater. The ripe fruit assumes a bright color in order to make it conspicuous among the green leaves and to make it attractive.

- The underside of the skin is therefore colorless (as on the orange), for color there is unnecessary. All fruits and vegetables are easier to peel when ripe.

- The peel is covered with a plastic coating to keep the fruit airtight and waterproof. (Only after peeling does the fruit begin to decay.) The peel correctly labels and identifies the contents, and the colors are labels which do not come off.

- The peel is disposable, for it eventually disintegrates and vanishes. It is also recyclable, for it turns into fertilizer for the soil.

## THOUGHT FOR TODAY:

Just as a fruit peel is designed to tell us there is a delicious fruit there, Hashem has designed us with free will, which can activate our abilities to succeed. When you can choose to rejoice with Hashem's gifts, Hashem will help you notice them more and experience more joy from them!

# Buds Are Gifts from Hashem

- The bud is a food miracle that comes out of the wood. These complicated mechanisms are produced by the tip of the twig; if you make an incision in the twig just below the bud, you only find plant juices.

- All beautiful things are designed with some form of protection. The sepal (green enclosure) encloses the bud and protects it until the flower opens.

- Plain wood can produce beautiful flowers and fruits. Thus the bud teaches us that ordinary-seeming people can produce great achievements from within themselves.

## THOUGHT FOR TODAY:

How can we grow happier in our lives? We can decide to look more and more for Hashem's gifts. New vistas will open daily and more gifts will begin to appear...

# Buds Are Gifts from Hashem
## (continued)

- As the bud matures, it dresses up in a lovely, cheerful, and inviting color to attract insects which pollinate it. The showy petals signal the presence of food and serve as convenient landing platforms.

- Patterns of lines and spots, called honey guides, lead insect visitors to the stores of nectar or pollen. Scent is another powerful attractant, especially on night-blooming species that would otherwise be difficult to find.

- All flowers have the function of producing seeds in order to perpetuate the species. All the parts of a flower contribute to its success as a reproductive structure. The flower petals signal the insects, the stamens (threadlike stalks with a sac on top) produce pollen grains that touch the insect. The pollen then descends down the tube to fertilize the egg cells, which then mature into a fruit that helps protect the seeds.

## THOUGHT FOR TODAY:

There may be flowers in front or back of your home that you never spent a minute to look at. View them as if they were an exquisite painting! Did you notice that they have magnificent colors? Did you hire an artist to come to paint them for you?

# Apples Are Gifts from Hashem

- The apple develops from the tissue of the flower that grew on the tree.

- Until the fruit becomes ripe, Hashem colors it green to render it unnoticeable among the green leaves, and also unattractive to the eater. As the fruit ripens, its color indicator gauges the degree of edibility, showing you the stage of ripeness and when you can anticipate eating it. The color is not merely a uniform red, but rather it is tinted like a beautiful painting.

- The apple ripens on the tree where it is exposed to the baking sun, which does just that: it bakes the apple to a perfect, delicious taste. The red color now sticks out like a red light proclaiming, "Stop! I am ready to be eaten! Enjoy me now!" Apples are also perfumed with an appetizing aroma.

- When ripe, the apple falls down to the eater below (teaching that gravity was also created to benefit people).

## THOUGHT FOR TODAY:

If you see an apple fall off a tree, don't just learn the law of gravity, learn the law of reality! Hashem created it for our benefit.

# Apples Are Gifts from Hashem
## (continued)

- The apple's juice is cunningly combined with the solid fruit so it does not spill out.

- The seeds are protected in a walled-in chamber so that after the contents of the apple are consumed, the eater finds a coupon entitling him to another package!

- The supporting stem is timed to become loose and easily detachable when the fruit becomes soft, juicy, sweet, and fragrant.

- The grass under the tree cushions the fall of the apple so that it does not get bruised.

- Apples have a tight-fitting, waterproof wrapper to protect them from rain and other elements. When the apple is peeled we see what a benefit the wrapper was. It is the best preserver for the fruit. It kept the fruit from decaying. After peeling, it disintegrates and recycles itself by dissolving into the soil.

- The main purpose of apples is pleasure (Tosfos, *Brachos* 37a). Hashem wishes to provide us with delicious foods to enjoy.

## THOUGHT FOR TODAY:

Buy an apple for this coming Shabbas to eat and enjoy. But do more than just eat it; set it on your table for ten minutes to view it and tell your family (and yourself) about it and why it reminds you to love Hashem.

# Oranges Are Gifts from Hashem

- As you bite an orange, the juice squirts in all directions. This fruit is really a container of juice that has been divided into individual sections which remain intact and which may be eaten separately.

- The orange has a thicker skin than the apple, as its meat is more liquid and requires better protection.

- The bright outer color serves to attract eaters, but the inside of the peel does not require any coloring since it is not normally visible.

- Orange seeds are bitter so that people will not eat them but rather throw them to where they can grow into more orange trees.

## THOUGHT FOR TODAY:

Set an orange beside an apple (or any other fruit) and contrast them. Observe that they have many differences, yet provide you with similar benefits.

# Watermelon Is a Gift from Hashem

- A watermelon is actually a prepackaged case of delicious juice. The liquid is uniformly distributed throughout the flesh so that it doesn't spill out when the melon is cut open.

- This fruit is protected by a thick, pulpy rind and doesn't have a bright-colored skin since it's designed for family feasts. The skin color urges patience until a group assembles. It's coated with the thinnest layer of deep green pigment to advertise the melon's ripeness.

- Watermelon seeds are coated with a slippery mucous that causes them to shoot out in all directions. They are also scattered throughout the melon, so that it is impossible to eat any part without spitting out some seeds.

- The beautiful red color stops at the watermelon rind. This color is obviously intended to enhance the pleasure of eating. (Why else would imitation foods use artificial food coloring, if not to deceive you into believing that they're the real thing?)

- It is therefore a kindness that the inner part of the rind is white to notify you to stop eating in order to avoid a stomachache.

## THOUGHT FOR TODAY:

Hashem provides us with many options to choose to practice our gratitude to Him. Don't just focus on one goal you think you may be missing in life, and forget to be grateful for the abundance of gifts Hashem is providing. Which do you like better: watermelon, peaches, apples, plums, bananas, kiwis, nectarines…?

# Dandelions Are Gifts from Hashem

- Once the dandelion's flower has served its function, the petals drop off and it prepares for the seed-ball stage.

- When the dandelion was in its flower stage, it was a short-stemmed plant. Now that it is in seed and needs to catch the wind so that its seeds can fly far away, the stem has grown so tall that the seed head stands high above the grass in the meadow.

- The tip of each piece of fluff acts as a serviceable parachute which transports the seed to where it will be planted. "He makes the winds His messengers" (Tehilim 104:4).

- The seed's parachute has about thirty delicate fluff hairs. They all grow apart and do not become entangled with each other. They stand with outstretched hairs and are ready to take off with the wind. These delicate fluff hairs are manufactured to be impervious to rain.

- The parachute becomes ready for flight only when its seed passenger has become ripe, because an unripe seed would not germinate and grow into a new plant.

## THOUGHT FOR TODAY:

One of the best methods for preparing for more fun and fulfillment in life is to deepen your gratitude for your current blessings. If a person isn't grateful for his current gifts, Hashem may say, "Why do you deserve more gifts?"

# Dandelions Are Gifts from Hashem (continued)

- The seed and parachute remain anchored until they are blown away. They then take off and fly aloft, even reaching mountaintops many miles away. The small seed passenger hangs from its parachute in perfect balance.

- A marvelous timing device loosens the seed when it is ripe and ready. It is not held too loosely, for it would then fall at the base of the plant instead of being blown far away to grow in a new place. It is also not held too tightly or it would resist the breeze. The seeds are just loose enough to remain attached to the plant until the wind detaches it, and off it goes into the world.

- The seed is enclosed in a strong, protective case to guard it against mishap until it comes to rest on fertile soil. There, it opens and begins the miraculous process of sending a tiny root down into the earth and stretching a tiny stem up toward the sun. This takes place whichever way the seed lands!

- This wild plant serves many useful functions. Thick growths of dandelions prevent soil erosion, and the tough, extensive root systems break up hard-packed earth. The deep roots lift valuable minerals (including precious trace elements) to the surface of the earth, where they eventually become available to other plants and animals, and man.

## THOUGHT FOR TODAY:

The dandelion teaches us that Hashem prepares gifts for us, ready to materialize as soon as we pray for them sincerely and do some *hishtadlus* (effort). Hashem is ready.

# Grass Is a Gift from Hashem

- Grass provides a soft cushion for sitting, reclining, or walking outdoors. It's natural carpeting!

- It provides pleasing color for the eyes. It also provides fragrance in the air and cools the atmosphere with the moisture of vegetation.

- It can become material for mats and clothing. Dry grass can be used as a fire starter and fuel.

- It prevents the formation of mud and dust.

- It provides food for livestock. Grass has a marvelous ability of spreading its seeds in order to grow all over. This insures an abundant supply of grazing grounds, even without man's efforts.

- Grass grows better than trees in many places because it requires less moisture. The major part of the grass plant, its roots, remains underground. Even in times of drought, grass can remain dormant and then revive itself when the rains return. In the winter, too, its root system is protected underground so that new shoots can sprout in the spring. After grazing animals nibble at blades of grass, the grass can grow again from their roots which remain underground.

## THOUGHT FOR TODAY:

You may have imitation grass/carpets in your home or office. Have you ever seen a carpet that replenishes itself each year?

# Food Production Is a Gift from Hashem

- To produce from utterly inedible, tasteless, and colorless earth an edible and tasty food is a miracle of miracles.

- The food we ingest would be a deadly poison if it were to enter our bloodstream directly, if not for the marvels upon marvels of chemical magic which metamorphoses the food into the thousands of products which actually feed the organs and tissues of our body.

## THOUGHT FOR TODAY:

> The *Sefer Hachinuch* explains that if we thank for food properly, sincerely, and wholeheartedly when saying Birchas Hamazon, we will also have plenty of food from Hashem when we need it.

## Your Belt Is a Gift from Hashem

- Consider the many holes in a belt so that it can be adjusted to the proper size. It is wide enough not to cause a welt.

- Many belts are constructed of genuine cowhide, which is sturdy and long lasting. It has a long-lasting metal buckle, which can also be transformed into a Shabbas-key belt.

- Besides the material benefits (support, comfort, and strength) the belt serves as a symbol that one must gird himself with added strength to remain firmly opposed to the wickedness of the outside world and the temptations of human nature. ("The belt is to separate between the heart and the lower body parts" [*Brachos* 24b].)

## THOUGHT FOR TODAY:

When we do a little bit, Hashem will do a lot to assist us. The fastest way to receive blessings from Hashem is to get busy doing our part while asking for His help.

# A Hat Is a Gift from Hashem

- A hat elevates the wearer, making him a head taller and more dignified. It is made to fit according to the head size.

- It is fashioned of comfortable cloth or felt, and it keeps the head warm and protected from cold, rain, or sunstroke.

- A man's black hat has a dignified outside band adorned with a bow. There is a lining inside and the brim is reinforced with stitching. It is dyed a pleasing color and it can withstand many rains.

- A head covering demonstrates that one is loyal and mindful of Hashem at all times. ("Cover your head so that you will be mindful of the fear of Heaven" [*Shabbas* 156b].) The head covering thereby crowns the wearer with true glory.

## THOUGHT FOR TODAY:

A hat shows that you are grateful to Hashem for giving you a head! We use our head (hopefully) all the time. Pray to Hashem to help you use it right.

# Seeds Are Gifts from Hashem

- A seed's color is inconspicuous so that it avoids attention and consumption. Its meat has no color or flavor for it does not need to tempt anyone.

- Apple seeds are discarded with the core. Watermelon seeds slide off the watermelon. Orange seeds are bitter so that the eater avoids them.

- The pits of the plum, peach, olive, cherry, and date are too hard even for nutcrackers, and the seed is therefore preserved for future generations. The seed casing is tougher than any other part of the tree.

- Some seeds have tiny forms of helicopters or parachutes attached to them. Maple seeds have wings to enable them to fly away from the parent tree's shade, to take root on their own.

- Evergreen tree cones bear seeds between their wooden scales. They are well protected until they mature and ripen. The seeds then fall to the ground and grow into new trees.

# THOUGHT FOR TODAY:

The potential of a huge tree is in a small seed. So too the goals you may want to achieve can be developed with Hashem's help. "On the path one desires to go, Hashem will lead him" (*Makos* 10b).

# Seeds Are Gifts from Hashem
## (continued)

- As milkweed dries, the seeds ripen and prepare to ride the wind. They soon fly away on their white plumes and colonize new sites for their species.

- One seed can produce hundreds and sometimes thousands of fruits!

- Each seed has its own store of food, contained in its jacket. This food is colorless and unsweetened, since the seed does not need an attractive color or luscious flavor to entice eaters. The seed's purpose is to avoid being eaten, to be planted, and to grow future fruits.

- The seed jacket is sturdy enough to protect its contents until they germinate, but when planted in soil it opens and begins to grow.

- The seed possesses machinery of vast scope and efficiency that transforms the simplest materials into the most complicated chemical products of countless varieties. All this is compressed into microscopic proportions to fit inside the seed.

## THOUGHT FOR TODAY:

When you plant a seed, you can grow a tree. This principle holds true in every area of life. When you give, you will receive. How much will you receive? It depends on how much you give. "According to the effort will be the reward" (*Avos* 5:23).

# Trees Are Gifts from Hashem

- Wood can be used for building materials or for fuel.

- Trees provide shade and coolness to freshen the atmosphere. Their foliage helps beautify the world.

- They retain the soil and prevent erosion and floods.

- Trees supply pulp for paper (books!) as well as various chemicals.

- They provide a home for birds' nests and a refuge for certain animals.

- When Avraham Avinu saw a tree, he saw a hotel where travelers could rest in the shade of the tree and eat of its fruit. He realized that that was Hashem's intended purpose for the tree and it became as clear to him as if there was an illuminated sign posted: "Hotel for wayfarers. All welcome!"

- The tree holds its leaves all summer while the sunlight works upon the chlorophyll and while the shade is desirable. However, during autumn, when the sunlight is limited and shade is no longer desirable, the leaves begin to fall.

- A tree's branches spread out on all sides, but not even one leaf is directly under the one above it! Hashem designed it this way intentionally so that each branch will be exposed to the maximum amount of sunlight and wind for its benefit.

## THOUGHT FOR TODAY:

> We learn from trees to welcome people with comforts and benefits. Provide an umbrella that offers shade and coolness. Give the best you can wherever you go, just as there are trees all over. Give a smile, say thank you... As we give kindness and love, we are emulating our Creator, who is always doing kindness for us.

# Thunder and Lightning Are Gifts from Hashem

- "His strength and power fill the world" (Blessing for Thunder).

- Lightning combines the nitrogen and oxygen of the air into nitrates, which fertilize the soil.

- Thunder warns people and animals to seek shelter while the lightning is at work (like a person with a red flag waving travelers away from a working area).

- A mighty thunder crash is expressly intended as a demonstration and reminder of the Creator's power: "Thunder straightens the crookedness of the heart — so that people should fear Him" (*Brachos* 59a).

## THOUGHT FOR TODAY:

Imagine if you received a FedEx gift package delivery from Hashem. Hashem sends us wake-up calls every now and then to teach us to appreciate our gifts from Hashem.

# Snow Is a Gift from Hashem

- "He Who gives snow like wool" (Tehilim 147:16).

- Its fluffy texture imprisons air just like wool, and it insulates the earth against frost, thus protecting the soil bacteria and the invaluable soil insects.

- The white color, like white wool, repels the sun's light and slows down the melting of the snow.

- The snow clings to mountainsides and melts gradually, bestowing the optimum benefit.

- The snow serves a double function: it is a blanket for the earth all winter, and in the spring the blanket melts gradually to water the soil.

## THOUGHT FOR TODAY:

Why does the snow in the winter look different than rain? The Talmud actually says that snow equals five rains, but why the change of color and texture? Hashem changes things to arouse our interest so that we should notice that He is the Master. He offers us many opportunities, in many guises, to see His work.

# Cows Are Gifts from Hashem

- A cow is a self-operating machine which transforms grass into milk, butter, cream, white cheese, yellow cheese, and even plastics (derived from casein and lactic acid). The grass is also transformed into cow meat and leather.

- Cattle can also be used to plow and draw wagons.

- The cow machine not only operates itself, but is also able to reproduce more machines of the same kind! When necessary, the machine can be transformed into food and clothing for its owner.

- A cow's horns serve to repel enemies.

- The teeth are specially designed for biting off and chewing grass.

- The spongy cartilage hoofs are made for long-lasting and shock-absorbing wear.

- The long, tufted tail is used as a flyswatter.

- The system of four stomachs and cud chewing are custom designed for the processing of tough grass fibers.

## THOUGHT FOR TODAY:

What a remarkable lesson! Hashem has created a unique machine that can utilize ordinary grass and transform it into food that humans can eat to live and thrive. So too Hashem has granted us the brains to create positives out of so-called negatives.

# Leaves Are Gifts from Hashem

- In every leaf, the heavily colored green side faces the sun and the pale green side is away from the sun. The chlorophyll-rich side faces upward, in order to utilize the sunlight.

- Each leaf is balanced in a horizontal position, to enable the leaf to receive the maximum sunlight.

- A tree's branches are spread on all sides, with none of them directly under the one above, in order to gain the maximum sunlight for the leaves — and the maximum shade for those who seek shelter under the tree.

- The leaf is coated with a transparent plastic which allows the sunlight to pass through, but which protects the leaf against the elements and against some chewing insects.

# THOUGHT FOR TODAY:

Leaves look like green paper money. Mishlai (11:28) teaches that righteous people think of wealth like leaves. Visualize that Hashem, who made the tree in front of your home grow thousands of leaves, can help you prosper with abundant wealth in other areas as well. "It is Hashem's blessing that provides wealth" (Mishlai 10:22).

# Leaves Are Gifts from Hashem
## (continued)

- The irregular outline of many species of leaves gives them a greater circumference, which facilitates the functions of the leaves.

- The leaves are crisscrossed with a network of veins that transport water and dissolved materials and act as a supporting frame for the lightweight fabric of the leaf.

- Each leaf is a food and material factory with the most intricate processes of production.

- The leaves are paper-thin to provide as much surface as possible while using as little material as possible.

## THOUGHT FOR TODAY:

Why are there so many small leaves? Hashem could have made a few large leaves. One answer is to teach us the principle of "one leaf at a time." The way to succeed in life is to do things gradually, step by step. "*Tafasta me'at tafasta*" — when you grab hold of a small amount you can succeed.

# Pollination Is a Gift from Hashem

- The flowering plant attracts insects by its nectar, color, and fragrance. The plant can't travel in order to transport its seeds to other plants, so it invites outside help by attracting insects to pollinate the species.

- The plant produces a sugary nectar as a reward for the bee's services. The bee cannot exist without the nectar and the flowers and fruit depend upon the bee for pollination.

- While the bee enjoys itself by crawling into the flower and sucking its nectar, it bumps into pollen-laden stamens which are strategically clustered around the flower's center near the nectar. The bee is well suited for the job due to its purposefully hairy body and legs, which become dusted with pollen to be carried onto the next plant.

- This system serves most of our fruit, vegetable, and flower crops, a total of about one hundred thousand species in all!

## THOUGHT FOR TODAY:

The system of pollination serves as a model for us to always look to serve others and to learn from them. "Who is wise? One who learns from every person" (Avos 4:1).

# SHAAR IV
# LIFE
# IS A GIFT FROM HASHEM

"There is always something to be grateful for. Why wait for later when you can be thankful now!"

# Mind and Memory Are Gifts from Hashem

- If not for forgetting, one would never be relieved of sorrow. No joy would expel sorrow from the mind, and nothing would cause a person pleasure, since he fully remembers the misfortunes of this world (*Chovos Halevavos, Bechina* 5). The wondrous process of temporarily removing information from the mind's consciousness (forgetting) cooperates with the faculty of memory.

- Many millions of pieces of information are stored away in the subconscious so as not to interfere with our active thoughts. When information is needed, the memory apparatus can cause old facts and pictures to leap out of the archives of the past and stand before our eyes. Sights, sounds, and smells are stored in the memory to be recalled and chosen when needed.

- Imagine: Without memory, you would not remember what belongs to you, what you received from others, what you saw, what you heard, what you said, what you were told, who was kind to you, who was mean to you, how to go back to a place. You would not remember what you read, and your past experiences would be useless in helping you for the future.

- "Without the quality of shame, people would not do kindness or refrain from evil" (*Chovos Halevavos*, Bechina 5).

- Most of all, thank Hashem for your normal mind!

## THOUGHT FOR TODAY:

*Hashem gave us the unique power of the mind to create an image of what we want. As we visualize our goal, we stimulate our senses to develop a firm, concrete desire which leads to, "In the path one is determined to go, Hashem will lead him" (Makos 10b).*

# Pain Is a Gift from Hashem

- The sensation of pain is an effective spur to seek healing. (People would neglect their teeth until they were irreparably decayed if not for the toothache which drives them to the dentist, who may be able to save the tooth.)

- The pains of the very old cause them to leave this life with less regret and ease their kin's bereavement upon their departure.

- Pain is also a message to the person to be humbled and improve his ways. (Just as he consults a physician, let him consult a Torah sage.)

- Pain also serves to remind one of the joys and miracles of normal well-being.

## THOUGHT FOR TODAY:

When we have challenges, we are being tested to see how we react. They are opportunities to help us strengthen our desire and determination. Every challenge is a blessing in disguise.

# Sickness Is a Gift from Hashem

- Fevers combat infection and also serve as a warning.

- A stomachache warns against overeating and against harmful foods.

- Fatigue forces a weary and distressed person to go to sleep to heal his body and mind by the magic medicine of slumber.

- Vomiting and diarrhea rid the body of harmful materials.

- One purpose of childhood illnesses is to train children that they should not place their trust blindly in this world (*Chovos Halevavos*).

## THOUGHT FOR TODAY:

We say this verse three times daily in Ashrai: "Hashem is good to all." Even pain, sickness or other discomfort is an aspect of His goodness.

# Suffering Is a Gift from Hashem

- "Hashem is kindly in all His deeds" (Tehilim 145:17). "Praiseworthy is the man whom You chastise, O G-d, and You teach him of Your Torah" (Tehilim 94:12). We have to learn to be grateful for these gifts of wisdom from Hashem!

- Similarly, in regard to entire nations, "Who chastises nations, is He not showing, is He not teaching knowledge?" (Tehilim 94:10).

- The vicissitudes of individuals and the upheavals of nations are designed by Hashem for the purpose of teaching knowledge. "The highest form of wisdom is the fear of G-d" (Tehilim 111:10). This wisdom is the most precious commodity there is, and its attainment is the main purpose of life.

# THOUGHT FOR TODAY:

Fulfilling the *mitzva* to say "*gam zu l'tovah*" (this too is for good) can actually change things to make them good and better, even spectacular.

# Suffering Is a Gift from Hashem
## (continued)

There are many lessons to be learned from suffering:

- One learns that his own fortune and well-being and the fortune of nations are not under human control, but rather Hashem is in control.

- One learns that this life is not the ultimate goal, it is merely a preparation for the afterlife. This lesson is especially effective when righteous men suffer, and even more so when the suffering is at the hands of the prosperous wicked. When this occurs, it is easier to feel that there is a Gehinnom prepared for the wicked oppressors and an eternal reward for the righteous that are being victimized.

- Suffering provides an impetus to repent and increase in piety, in order to arouse Hashem's mercy.

- Through suffering, one achieves the great quality of humility. By justifying Hashem and accepting the blame on ourselves, we achieve greatness. "Let us search and examine our ways, and return to G-d" (Aicha 3:40). It thus serves as an impetus to self-searching and self-betterment.

## THOUGHT FOR TODAY:

We are not able to see everything in our future, but Hashem, the Supreme Creator and Provider of all, does see every option. Hashem delivers the best in ways that at times surprise us: "How is this going to turn out good for me? Thank you, Hashem, for your gifts!"

# Suffering Is a Gift from Hashem
## (continued)

Within each kind of suffering is a gift from Hashem.

- **Poverty:** One is freed from the worries money causes, and from many obligations toward Hashem and people that wealthy people are held responsible for.

- **Monotony:** Happiness of peaceful existence.

- **Results of overindulgence:** A lesson to teach one temperance and self-control in matters of food and beverages, and not to neglect one's health and safety.

- **Results of anger, envy, wrong behavior to others, and willful waste of property:** A lesson to teach proper *midos* (character development).

- **Unhappiness resulting from the endless pursuit after pleasure:** To teach one to refrain from trying to satisfy his desires for pleasure or money, which can never really be accomplished. One should rather work on training himself to "rejoice with your lot" (*Avos* 4:1).

# THOUGHT FOR TODAY:

One of the purposes of poverty is to prompt a person to ask himself, "What does Hashem want from me? Can my free will change my situation?" To some degree, each person can create the life he wants. Every person has the option to change his thoughts and pray to Hashem for help to change everything.

# Suffering Is a Gift from Hashem
## (continued)

- **Body pain:** An indicator that the body needs repair, and that the soul is in danger. A double kindness!

- **Disabilities of old age:** Gradual retirement from this world to remind a person to repent and prepare for the World to Come. These also ease the family's sufferings upon his departure.

- **Death:** Entranceway to the greatest of benefits in the afterlife.

- **Suffering in Gehinnom:** Purification to prepare one for eternal happiness.

- **Early death:** Sometimes to spare one from sufferings that are imminent.

- **When children die young:** "G-d teaches them in the afterlife" (*Avodah Zarah* 3b; *Rashi*).

- **Work:** "Idleness leads to mental instability" (*Kesubos* 59b).

## THOUGHT FOR TODAY:

One of the famous questions is, why does it seem that some righteous people suffer, whereas some wicked people seem to prosper? Rabbi Miller, *zt"l*, explained that when we learn how to think, we may discover that a lot of what people perceive is merely illusions. What some think is a righteous person suffering may actually be a wicked person prospering!

# Poverty Is a Gift from Hashem

- "Hashem examined all good gifts to give to the Jewish nation, and He found nothing better than poverty" (*Chagigah* 9b). Poverty frees a person from

  - Arrogance;

  - The great error of thinking that this life is our ultimate purpose;

  - Thinking that our good fortune depends solely on our efforts and talents;

  - Overlooking one's faults.

- A poor person has thereby a golden opportunity to acquire the gems of True Knowledge; lack of wealth is a small price to pay for this most precious of possessions. Let us practice saying to Hashem, "Thank You, O G-d, that You were angry with me" (*Yeshaya* 12:1).

## THOUGHT FOR TODAY:

By not having more money, many people have learned to discover inner resources which led them to become great and produce large amounts of wealth as well.

# History Is a Gift from Hashem

- By examining his past history, every person can discover a great network of intricate plan and purpose, which makes him aware of Hashem's constant guidance of his footsteps.

- Similarly, by examining the events of mankind's history, one becomes aware of Hashem's guidance of the affairs of nations.

- A misfortune is a message and summons to repentance. A stroke of good fortune is an indication of a good deed that was done. Hashem gives a clue — measure for measure — to indicate the cause of the event. "When one sees misfortunes coming upon him, let him search into his deeds" (*Brachos* 5a).

- History brings us to realize that we have been protected and guided by Hashem as a nation in exile for so long!

## THOUGHT FOR TODAY:

Looking back to our past is one of the best ways to fulfill "Who is wise? One who sees the future!" (*Tamid* 32a). The past can guide us to prepare properly for the future.

# History Is a Gift from Hashem
## (continued)

- Three times in our history we had a leader who was the greatest Torah sage of his time and who simultaneously had great wealth and power: Moshe Rabbainu, Rabbi Yehuda Hanasi, and Rav Ashi (*Gitin* 59a). These three periods in history were crucial for three major stages relating to the Torah: the giving of the Torah through Moshe, the closing of the Mishnah by Rebbi, and the sealing of the Talmud by Rav Ashi.

- "When fortune befalls a vessel on the seas, the dwellers in caves, and even entire nations, it is because of Israel" (*Yevamos* 63a). These fortunes occur either to encourage the Jewish nation, to protect them and their livelihood, to teach them some truth, or to warn them to improve their ways.

- The destruction of the first sanctuary and of the second one almost five hundred years later took place in the same month and on the same day! (A sign of the Divine guidance of our affairs.)

- In 5252 the Jews were expelled from Spain, and in that same year Columbus discovered America, which became the most influential Jewish community since Spain.

- The job (or *shidduch*, etc.) you thought was just for you, fell through, and then a much better offer came along, which was obviously what Hashem had in mind for you!

## THOUGHT FOR TODAY:

> The more we thank Hashem for His gifts to us, the more we merit to receive more from Him. You can change your own history by choosing to think thoughts of self-improvement and *teshuva*.

# Animals Are Gifts from Hashem

- Camels have short tails so that they will not get entangled in the abundance of thorns in their desert habitat.

- The ox has a long tail to swat flies.

- Locusts' antennae are soft and pliable so they do not crack when the locust jumps between the stiff blades of reed grass. Our ears have the same pliability for the same purpose: to be flexible when a person lies down (*Shabbas* 77b).

- The chicken's eyelid closes upward instead of downward (like a human eyelid). The chicken usually perches itself on high places, where harmful smoke may reach it. Because the eyelid closes upward, rising smoke does not enter the chicken's eye (*Shabbas* 77b).

## THOUGHT FOR TODAY:

Animals that have tails do not generally have arms, hands, and fingers like we do. We can use a fly swatter to chase away flies; animals have tails. Everything in life has a plan and purpose. When we learn to appreciate Hashem's gifts to us, we will always be happy for everything we see in general and for each specific benefit.

# Animals Are Gifts from Hashem
## (continued)

- Camels have humps, accumulated fat which serves as a reserve when food and water are scarce in the camel's desert habitat. Thus, a camel can travel for several days without drinking.

- There is a species of ravens that refuses to feed its offspring. Hashem, therefore, causes worms to develop from the dung deposits of the parent bird. These worms nourish the young ravens (*Kesubos* 49b).

- The walrus has two elongated teeth (two feet long) which it can use as a defense weapon, or as an ice pick and chisel in order to provide for itself.

- The anteater's tongue is two feet long. It functions like flypaper; it is coated with a sticky glue that catches ants deep within their underground home.

# THOUGHT FOR TODAY:

Why are your teeth not longer, like a bear's? Why is your tongue not longer, like a dog's? Hashem has equipped you perfectly for your needs!

# Animals Are Gifts from Hashem
## (continued)

- When the puffer fish senses danger, it quickly inflates its body by gulping in air or water to create a sudden, dramatic change in size so as to scare away would-be attackers. As soon as the danger passes, the puffer deflates itself.

- The giraffe, the tallest land animal, has a long neck in order to enable it to eat tree leaves that grow fifteen feet above the ground.

- The elephant's long trunk is used mainly for picking up food. It is a unique, miraculous structure which serves as an arm to handle objects as big as a tree or as small as a peanut.

- The elephant's trunk also serves as a drinking hose, a showerhead with which it sprinkles itself with water, for smelling purposes, to steer its young, and to chastise its young.

## THOUGHT FOR TODAY:

Why is a giraffe's neck so long? Hashem could have made the neck shorter. We learn from unusual creatures that Hashem can do anything and everything. He is infinite, with all the power, wisdom, and kindness to do everything right with good reasons.

# Animals Are Gifts from Hashem
## (continued)

- "They chased after you like bees…" (Devarim 1:44). "As a bee which dies as soon as it stings a person [because its sting is barbed and cannot be withdrawn; after it stings once, it falls dead]" (Rashi, ibid.). The bee can protect itself, which is a necessity for the security of its beehive. However, to prevent it from taking the offensive and turning into a menace, Hashem designed it to destroy itself when it uses its weapon.

- When an opossum is attacked by certain predators, it has a unique method of saving itself. The animal lapses into a simulated state of unconsciousness. Its tongue hangs out; it lies still; the limbs become stiff without apparent sensation; and it appears as if it has suddenly dropped dead. This "dead" act is the last thing the predator expects, and the bewildered animal seeks food elsewhere.

- A lizard also needs protection from the desert heat. Hashem has therefore covered its entire body with scales. They form a tile-like coat that conserves moisture and protects the animal against predators. Certain species have scaly crests or fans that can be raised in threat displays to frighten an attacker. Other lizards have webbing on their feet that act like snowshoes, thus permitting these reptiles to easily run atop loose, shifting sand.

- The wolf has scent glands in its feet that emit odors when the wolf scratches its feet. As the wolf travels about, it leaves scent messages along the way. Later, other wolves smell these odors and interpret the messages. Fresh scent marks mean that there may be some food available. The younger wolves usually follow in that direction, while older wolves search for prey in different directions. Hashem has provided these animals with effective coded messages to use in many ways. They ward off intruders, find their way, and know when other animals have been nearby, through scent messages.

## THOUGHT FOR TODAY:

From each amazing creature Hashem created, we learn lessons on how we can serve Him better. We need to ask ourselves, what does Hashem want me to learn from this creature?

Bees, for example, have stingers and produce honey. People who go for the honey may end up getting stung. This teaches us that when we turn to people for favors, we end up "owing them one"; they may say, "Now I need you to do this for me." Thus it is always best to pray to Hashem for all of our needs. He is the One to turn to.

# Animals Are Gifts from Hashem
## (continued)

- A deer is designed for running. Its lungs and windpipe are large, and its hooves are divided and angled so it can run on tiptoes, allowing for greater speed, traction, and maneuverability. A deer's heart is twice the size of that of other animals that weigh the same amount. The deer can run at top speeds of forty to sixty miles per hour in short bursts, and at a sustained pace of thirty miles per hour. As a survival technique, the animal prefers to flee rather than attempt to fight.

- A woodpecker is able to hammer holes in trees without suffering from headaches because it has extra thick bones in its head and strong neck muscles to protect it from concussions. Hashem designed this bird with all of the equipment necessary for drilling hole-nests in trees. It has a chisel-edged beak, a stiff tail used to brace itself against the tree while drilling, and sharp, curved jaws with which to grip the tree's rough bark.

- Hashem has bestowed the flounder with an incredible ability to match the color and pattern of its background. It expands and contracts its skin color cells to vary the amount of pigment that shows on its skin. The flounder is thereby able to imitate a light, sandy surface; a dark, muddy surface; a mottled, gravelly background; and anything in between.

## THOUGHT FOR TODAY:

*"Run like a deer to do the will of your Father in heaven" (Avos 5:20). Hashem has given us the ability to run quickly to do what we desire.*

# Animals Are Gifts from Hashem
## (continued)

- Since a tiger spends much of the year among tall, dry grass and reeds, its dark, striped fur enables it to blend in with its surroundings in order to conceal it from its prey.

- What does an octopus do when it is attacked by a predator? It squirts out a dark, thick mass of ink in the form of a blob roughly the size and shape of its body. At the same time, the octopus itself becomes pale and propels itself to safety while its assailant continues to attack the dark cloud.

- Why is the snowshoe rabbit's fur white in the winter but brown in the summer? Hashem causes the hairs to change color in order for them to blend in with the winter snow and the summer vegetation. The rabbit is thereby difficult to detect and protected from its predators.

## THOUGHT FOR TODAY:

"Do not separate from others" (*Avos* 4:7). It is essential that a Jew live together with other Torah- and *mitzva*-observant Jews. Thus we learn to blend in with others, not to be apart from the *frum* community.

# Animals Are Gifts from Hashem
## (continued)

- How are snakes mobile without feet? They glide forward by moving the scales on their undersides forward and up, one section at a time. To move more quickly, they twist into S-shaped curves, affording them more leverage and speed.

- Young mammals are nourished by their mothers' milk, which is exactly suited to their particular needs. A seal's milk is more than 50 percent fat in order to enable the pup's development of an insulating layer of blubber to protect it in the frigid sea. A camel's milk is 87 percent water, thus designed by Hashem in order to provide additional fluid for its existence in dry deserts. The kangaroo rat, which also lives in dry places but is active only at night, produces milk with only a 50 percent water content.

- Human milk is exactly suited to the needs of human offspring. Researchers have called it Hashem's gift to babies: it is super-nutritious, hygienic, and full of antibodies that help immunize the child against infection. Milk of mothers whose babies are premature is unique to protect them against afflictions unique to preemies.

## THOUGHT FOR TODAY:

Each creature has exactly what it needs, when it needs it. "Hashem is good to all" (Ashrai). Keep thinking about Hashem's goodness every day.

"Hashem saw all that He had made and behold, it was very good!" (Beraishis 1:3!)

# Animals Are Gifts from Hashem
## (continued)

- How does a mosquito collect its food from humans and animals (preferably animals)? A mosquito can hover in midair, move vertically, and even fly backward in search of potential prospects. It then utilizes its proboscis (flexible, projecting nose) to drill beneath the surface of the skin in search of a supply of blood. Its proboscis consists of six different shafts: four are cutting and piercing tools; the fifth transports blood from the host to the mosquito; the sixth transports saliva.

- The mosquito was perfectly designed by Hashem to drill and pump its food supply in order to survive. Humans, in turn, are served by mosquitos, for they provide a plentiful source of protein (14,000 mosquitos per acre) for birds, fish, and other insects.

- The eagle depends on sight more than on any other sense, and it has better eyesight than any other animal. Its eyes are very large, and they contain many special cells which enable the eagle to perceive detail even at great distances.

The eagle can spot a fish from about a mile away. It then swiftly zeroes in on its prey while continuously refocusing its eyes as it comes closer and the prey continues to move. (Similarly, a person must train his eyes to look for food, i.e., that which will enhance and sustain his body and soul. At the same time, he should be prepared to swiftly turn away from harmful sights.)

- An archerfish uses water as a weapon to shoot its prey. The fish cruises near the surface close to shore, looking for spiders, insects, and the like on overhanging branches. When it sights a potential meal, it spits out a burst of water at the target, causing the victim to fall into the stream. The archerfish is usually accurate at distances of about four feet.

# THOUGHT FOR TODAY:

*We can find many good lessons in every creature Hashem created.*

# Animals Are Gifts from Hashem
## (continued)

- The crab has a tight-fitting shell which does not grow along with its body. Hashem designed the crab to break out of its skin and form a new skin in order to grow. First, its body absorbs much of the calcium from its shell. This calcium is used to stiffen the soft layer of skin underneath the shell. The blood then flows from the pincers back into the body, causing them to shrink in order to fit through the passageway of the old shell. The animal then backs out of its skeleton through a slit across its back, leaving the old shell in a single piece. Amazing!

- Insects have compound eyes made up of separate units with separate lenses. They therefore perceive the world differently than humans do. They can detect motion much better than humans and are thus equipped to avoid predators and to track down prey. They do not see shapes well, for they have no need to analyze the essence of that which they see.

- Hashem designed the jellyfish with a system that is able to pump water into its belly and then contract in order to force the water out. As the water is expelled in one direction, the jellyfish is propelled in the opposite direction.

## THOUGHT FOR TODAY:

*From the shell of a crab and other such creatures we learn that our bodies are not the essence of who we are! The neshama which Hashem blew into us is the pure core of our identity. We are a portion of the Divine and our outside form is secondary and changing.*

# SHAAR V
# BEING JEWISH IS A GIFT FROM HASHEM

"The more we think about gratitude, the happier we become!"

# Torah Is the Greatest Gift from Hashem

- There is no good that compares to Torah! (*Avos* 6:3). The greatest benefit that Hashem bestowed on us is the Torah… which was given to us through Moshe His prophet… (*Chovos Halevavos* 2:5).

- The Torah sets us apart from the nations and distinguishes us as a nation of leaders and holy people.

- It confers dignity upon us and causes us to abstain from degenerate pastimes. It also prevents the waste of our property.

- It protects our health and safety and confers to us mental equilibrium.

- It brings peace in the home and community, and it causes us to respect the good and abhor the contemptible.

# THOUGHT FOR TODAY:

Torah is called "light" (Mishlai 6:23). Imagine a clear, beautiful day of illuminating, sparkling light that permeates the whole wide world with pure, spiritual energy. It lights every part of Hashem's universe and it lights up every cell of our bodies. "Torah study exceeds all" (*Peah* 1:1).

# Torah Is a Gift from Hashem
## (continued)

- It makes us mindful of the Creator, and many other benefits of which the Giver of the Torah is aware. Of all the benefits for which one must be grateful to Hashem, the greatest is Torah study. This is the sole precept and the sole pleasure for which a preliminary *brachah* is required by the Torah.

- We must thank Hashem always, for making us the seed of Israel and for the Torah He gave us, which causes our excellence. We must also thank Him for preserving and multiplying us, for the wondrous deeds He has done for us, and for the countless benefits that He has bestowed on us.

- In addition, we thank Him for the glorious future which Hashem promised our fathers that He would give us. May the Almighty help us serve Him and recognize His goodness, mercy, and kindness.

## THOUGHT FOR TODAY:

The Torah is called the *kli chemda*, the most desirable entity there is. Hashem used it for creating the universe. It served as the blueprint of creation and it is the manual for maintaining the universe. The Torah teaches us how to live with the 613 primary *mitzva* principles of life and connection to Hashem.

# Shabbas Is a Gift from Hashem

**"A song for the day of Shabbas" (Tehilim 92).**

This song does not actually mention the word *Shabbas* after the introductory verse. Nevertheless this psalm is the very essence of Shabbas, for it speaks about the Creation of the universe.

One of the main purposes of Shabbas is to appreciate the Creation by the Creator. The Shabbas day should be especially devoted to the study of this subject. (Some people read some pages of this book every Shabbas.)

**"It is good to give thanks [and praise] to G-d, to sing to Your name, O Most High!"**

- "It is good…" This does not mean that it is *also* good. The true meaning is: The *highest* goodness is to give thanks and sing to Hashem. The reason for this is because Hashem "built the world in kindliness" (Tehilim 89:3). He declared the world good, and very good: "G-d saw all that He made, and behold it was very good" (Beraishis 1:31). We must therefore thank Him and sing His praises for all the phenomena of the universe which are all *very good*.

- "To His name," because we are unable to praise Him accurately, for He is too exalted for us to be able to describe Him. However, we know His name (*shem*, derived from *shamoa*, to hear), for we have heard of His deeds and we see His handiwork.

- "Most High." He is the cause and the motivator of all good that comes to us.

## THOUGHT FOR TODAY:

Gratitude to Hashem is described as the greatest of virtues and the one which leads to all other attributes.

# Shabbas Is a Gift from Hashem
## (continued)

**"It is good to relate at length in the morning Your kindliness, and in the evenings Your steadfastness" (Tehilim 92).**

- From the beginning and until the end of the day, this is the best career and the highest good for a person: to relate at length the kindliness of Your creations and Your steadfastness in maintaining it.

- "On the ten-string and on the viol, with meditation of the harp." Every form of expression should be utilized in order to gain the fullest understanding of the infinite kindliness of creation. External means are an additional stimulus to aid the mind. "The exteriority awakens the interiority" (*Mesilas Yesharim* 7).

- "For You make me happy with Your work; I sing at the deeds of Your hands." Deeds include those related in the Torah, those handed down by historical tradition, and also those deeds that our eyes see, which include the entire universe. The study of the Creator's handiwork causes joy which engenders gratitude to the Creator.

- We say in the Shabbas prayers, "Those who keep Shabbas rejoice in Your kingship," for His kingship means that everything that exists or transpires is benevolently purposeful! This understanding of creation and the reflection in the wisdom and kindliness of creation bring to a joyous Jew all forms of happiness; "A good heart is at an everlasting feast" (Mishlai 15:15).

## THOUGHT FOR TODAY:

The key to happiness is to rejoice with our portions (Avos 4:1). By recognizing that Hashem created His world for each of us, we will always be rejoicing! The Talmud declares, "Every individual is obligated to say: Because of me, Hashem created the world!" (Sanhedrin 37a)

# Shabbas Is a Gift from Hashem
## (continued)

**"How great are Your deeds, Hashem; how very deep are Your thoughts [plans]!" (Tehillim 92)**

- Each of His deeds is so great as to serve by itself as an incontrovertible testimony to Hashem's greatness. In addition, the profundity of His plans is infinite. Every component and every particle of the universe was created with the full measure of the Creator's wisdom. This study should be the great purpose of our existence: to study and appreciate the Creator's handiwork.

**"The ignorant man does not know, and a fool does not understand this."**

- Many miss this great opportunity to discover Hashem's greatness and kindness.

**"When the wicked grow like grass, and all the evildoers sprout."**

- At times the wicked even seem to prosper. Their literature and institutions fill the world with falsehood. But the end will be "they shall be destroyed forever." Their seeming success is merely a temporary illusion.

- "You, O Lord, shall be Most High forever." All who rise up against the true G-d or against the Jewish nation, who are called Hashem's nation which testifies for the true G-d, shall go lost.

## THOUGHT FOR TODAY:

The goodness of Hashem's world is the true reality which we need to recognize and live with. Thus this is the day for singing about Hashem's goodness, to remind ourselves of how fortunate we are. His goodness is all around us to appreciate and enjoy!

# Shabbas Is a Gift from Hashem
## (continued)

**"For behold Your enemies, O Lord, behold Your enemies shall go lost; all the evildoers shall fall apart" (Tehilim 92).**

- Even their temporary prosperity is merely for the purpose of compensating them for their few merits in order to destroy them afterward.

**"The righteous one shall blossom like the date tree; like the cedar of Levanon he shall grow great."**

- By utilizing his life for the study of Hashem's deeds, the virtuous person produces the fruits of True Knowledge, and he comes to a greatness which elevates him above his generation. This, however, is best accomplished when he begins as a youth...

**"Planted in the house of the Lord; in the courtyards of our G-d they blossom."**

- As one persists in observing the phenomena of creation, and even the very same phenomena, day after day, he will come to a deep and full Awareness of the Creator.

**"They shall continue to produce fruit in their old age; they shall be full of vigor and flourishing."**

- This career of rejoicing in Hashem's handiwork, if begun early and continued throughout the years, shall give us the vigor and freshness which come from true happiness, even into old age. "Sages, as they grow older, their wisdom increases" (*Shabbas* 152a).

## THOUGHT FOR TODAY:

*Shabbas gives us new eyes. Look with grateful eyes; only see Hashem's goodness.*

# Rosh Chodesh Is a Gift from Hashem

- The benediction of the new moon includes the following statement: "To the moon He said it should renew itself, as a crown of glory to those who are carried from birth [the Jewish people, as in Yeshaya 46:3]; for they are destined to be renewed just as she is." This is the meaning of the verse in Beraishis (1:14): "May there be luminaries in the expanse of the heavens to divide between the day and the night; they shall be for signs, and appointed times, and for days, and for years."

- The "times" refer to the special holidays Hashem has designated for the Jews, as the Torah states, "the appointed times of G-d" (Vayikra 23:4). Similarly, "signs" refers to this message of the new moon. The sages understood that among the purposes of the moon's phases is this prominent message to honor and encourage the Jewish nation.

# THOUGHT FOR TODAY:

One of the purposes of Rosh Chodesh is to thank Hashem for a gift of a new month. Rabbi Miller, zt"l, said:

- Thank Hashem for the month that has passed,

- Say you're sorry for not appreciating Hashem's gifts sufficiently,

- Pray for a new month of life so that you should enjoy the incredible gifts Hashem is bestowing on you.

# SHAAR VI
# THE MORNING BLESSINGS AND YOUR GIFTS FROM HASHEM

"Giving is true getting, and blessing is receiving!"

# Why We Say Blessings

"The heavens are for Hashem, and the earth He gave to man" (Tehilim 115:16).

"The heavens are for Hashem." This refers to before one says blessings. "The earth He gave to man." This refers to after one says blessings.

— *Brachos 35a*

- It is forbidden for a person to benefit from the pleasures of this world without first making a *brachah*. A *brachah* is the minimum payment for anything, an expression of thanks for the benefit one is receiving from Hashem.

- The word *brachah* is derived from the word *berech* (knee), which suggests humble gratitude. One should feel "weighed down" with gratitude to Hashem for the benefits he receives.

- We have a daily list of blessings (Birchos Hashachar) in which we thank Hashem for many specific benefits. These *brachos* are required for men and women (see *Mishnah Berurah* 70:2 and *Aruch Hashulchan* 70:21).

## THOUGHT FOR TODAY:

We think it is "normal" to wake up in the morning, to sit up, stand up, and walk around. The truth is each step is a great gift from Hashem. The *brachos* we say serve to train us to develop an awareness throughout the day to pay attention to Hashem's gifts to us. Every time we say a heartfelt *brachah*, we accomplish many great *mitzvos* of loving, thanking, and serving Hashem.

# "He has commanded us regarding washing the hands…"

- We wash our hands in preparation for our service of Hashem, similar to a *kohen* serving in the Bais Hamikdash.

- Our hands are very useful (see page 75). They are a unique gift from Hashem, thus we thank Him for the great gift of being able to use our hands.

בָּרוּךְ אַתָּה ה' אֱלֹהֵינוּ מֶלֶךְ הָעוֹלָם, אֲשֶׁר קִדְּשָׁנוּ בְּמִצְוֹתָיו וְצִוָּנוּ עַל נְטִילַת יָדָיִם:

# Asher Yatzar

## "... Who has formed a person with wisdom..."

- Our physical body is full of miraculous wonders.

- Each component of the body is more complicated than a huge skyscraper with all its details of steel framework, masonry, plumbing, ventilation, lighting, hardware, fixtures, and furniture.

  "... and created within him many openings [mouth, nose, and the openings that emit body wastes] and many hollow organs [heart, stomach, intestines]..."

- The many orifices must function constantly in a certain fashion for the person to be healthy.

- We should consider separately the opening and closing of each organ, and thank Hashem for the mouth, nose, heart, stomach...

## "Blessed are You, Hashem, the Healer of all flesh..."

- The emission of body waste is crucial to a person's survival.
- This process is like many complicated surgical operations which Hashem has built in to the body as automatic systems.

## "...Who works wondrously."

- The system through which the nutrients are selected and separated from the food, while the wastes are rejected and expelled from the body, is a wonder of wonders.
- This blessing is therefore an all-encompassing thanks to Hashem for the wonders of our body and our physical health.

**Thank Hashem for your body.**

בָּרוּךְ אַתָּה ה', אֱלֹהֵינוּ מֶלֶךְ הָעוֹלָם, אֲשֶׁר יָצַר אֶת הָאָדָם בְּחָכְמָה. וּבָרָא בוֹ נְקָבִים נְקָבִים. חֲלוּלִים חֲלוּלִים. גָּלוּי וְיָדוּעַ לִפְנֵי

כִּסֵּא כְבוֹדֶךָ, שֶׁאִם יִסָּתֵם אֶחָד מֵהֶם, אוֹ אִם יִפָּתֵחַ אֶחָד מֵהֶם, אִי אֶפְשָׁר לְהִתְקַיֵּם אֲפִלּוּ שָׁעָה אֶחָת. בָּרוּךְ אַתָּה ה', רוֹפֵא כָל-בָּשָׂר וּמַפְלִיא לַעֲשׂוֹת:

**Nusach Sefard:**

בָּרוּךְ אַתָּה ה' אֱלֹהֵינוּ מֶלֶךְ הָעוֹלָם אֲשֶׁר יָצַר אֶת הָאָדָם בְּחָכְמָה וּבָרָא בוֹ נְקָבִים נְקָבִים חֲלוּלִים חֲלוּלִים. גָּלוּי וְיָדוּעַ לִפְנֵי כִסֵּא כְבוֹדֶךָ שֶׁאִם יִפָּתֵחַ אֶחָד מֵהֶם אוֹ יִסָּתֵם אֶחָד מֵהֶם אִי אֶפְשָׁר לְהִתְקַיֵּם וְלַעֲמוֹד לְפָנֶיךָ: בָּרוּךְ אַתָּה ה' רוֹפֵא כָל בָּשָׂר וּמַפְלִיא לַעֲשׂוֹת:

# Thanking for the Torah

We include in our thanks to Hashem three major elements concerning Torah study:

- **The toil and labor** in Torah, without which it is impossible to know the Torah (*Megilah* 6b).

- **The delight and pleasure** of Torah study. "Please make the words of Your Torah pleasant in our mouths."

- **This tremendous gift** was given **exclusively** to us!

**Thank Hashem for the Torah.**

בָּרוּךְ אַתָּה ה', אֱלֹהֵינוּ מֶלֶךְ הָעוֹלָם, אֲשֶׁר קִדְּשָׁנוּ בְּמִצְוֹתָיו וְצִוָּנוּ לַעֲסוֹק בְּדִבְרֵי תוֹרָה:

וְהַעֲרֶב נָא ה' אֱלֹהֵינוּ אֶת דִּבְרֵי תוֹרָתְךָ בְּפִינוּ וּבְפִיּוֹת עַמְּךָ בֵּית יִשְׂרָאֵל. וְנִהְיֶה אֲנַחְנוּ וְצֶאֱצָאֵינוּ (וְצֶאֱצָאֵי צֶאֱצָאֵינוּ) וְצֶאֱצָאֵי עַמְּךָ בֵּית יִשְׂרָאֵל כֻּלָּנוּ יוֹדְעֵי שְׁמֶךָ וְלוֹמְדֵי תוֹרָתְךָ לִשְׁמָהּ. בָּרוּךְ אַתָּה ה', הַמְלַמֵּד תּוֹרָה לְעַמּוֹ יִשְׂרָאֵל:

בָּרוּךְ אַתָּה ה', אֱלֹהֵינוּ מֶלֶךְ הָעוֹלָם, אֲשֶׁר בָּחַר בָּנוּ מִכָּל הָעַמִּים וְנָתַן לָנוּ אֶת תּוֹרָתוֹ. בָּרוּךְ אַתָּה ה', נוֹתֵן הַתּוֹרָה:

**Nusach Sefard and Edot Hamizrach:**

בָּרוּךְ אַתָּה ה', אֱלֹהֵינוּ מֶלֶךְ הָעוֹלָם, אֲשֶׁר קִדְּשָׁנוּ בְּמִצְוֹתָיו וְצִוָּנוּ עַל דִּבְרֵי תוֹרָה:

וְהַעֲרֶב נָא ה' אֱלֹהֵינוּ אֶת דִּבְרֵי תוֹרָתְךָ בְּפִינוּ וּבְפִיפִיּוֹת עַמְּךָ בֵּית יִשְׂרָאֵל. וְנִהְיֶה אֲנַחְנוּ וְצֶאֱצָאֵינוּ וְצֶאֱצָאֵי צֶאֱצָאֵינוּ כֻּלָּנוּ יוֹדְעֵי שְׁמֶךָ וְלוֹמְדֵי תוֹרָתְךָ לִשְׁמָהּ. בָּרוּךְ אַתָּה ה', הַמְלַמֵּד תּוֹרָה לְעַמּוֹ יִשְׂרָאֵל:

בָּרוּךְ אַתָּה ה', אֱלֹהֵינוּ מֶלֶךְ הָעוֹלָם, אֲשֶׁר בָּחַר בָּנוּ מִכָּל הָעַמִּים וְנָתַן לָנוּ אֶת תּוֹרָתוֹ. בָּרוּךְ אַתָּה ה', נוֹתֵן הַתּוֹרָה:

## "Hashem, the soul which You gave me is pure…"

- When a person wakes up, he not only regains his consciousness and his ability to move, but he is like one who is actually reborn with a renewed body and mind.

- We thank Hashem daily for this process and for this hint to the future *techiyas hamaisim* (revival of the dead), which will be for an eternal existence of happiness.

- A human soul is great beyond fathoming, for it comes from the Creator and reflects His endless greatness: "He blew into his nostrils the breath of life" (Beraishis 2:7); "One who blows, blows of himself" (*Ramban*, ibid.).

**Thank Hashem for your Divine soul, which is so great that you should appreciate that you are greater than a genius!**

אֱלֹהַי נְשָׁמָה שֶׁנָּתַתָּ בִּי טְהוֹרָה הִיא
אַתָּה בְרָאתָהּ אַתָּה יְצַרְתָּהּ אַתָּה נְפַחְתָּהּ

בִּי וְאַתָּה מְשַׁמְּרָהּ בְּקִרְבִּי וְאַתָּה עָתִיד לִטְּלָהּ מִמֶּנִּי וּלְהַחֲזִירָהּ בִּי לֶעָתִיד לָבֹא כָּל זְמַן שֶׁהַנְּשָׁמָה בְקִרְבִּי מוֹדֶה אֲנִי לְפָנֶיךָ ה' אֱלֹהַי וֵאלֹהֵי אֲבוֹתַי רִבּוֹן כָּל הַמַּעֲשִׂים אֲדוֹן כָּל הַנְּשָׁמוֹת. בָּרוּךְ אַתָּה ה', הַמַּחֲזִיר נְשָׁמוֹת לִפְגָרִים מֵתִים:

# "Thank You, Hashem… for giving the rooster/the mind understanding to distinguish between day and night."

- One word for the human mind (heart) is *sechvi*, which also means a rooster. We therefore correlate the two, and thank Hashem for supplying us with a creature that can be used to wake us up, and with a system that registers the difference between day and night.

- We proclaim that this world is not a place in which to sleep away one's life; we need to achieve in Torah and *mitzvos* and dispel the darkness.

- Without the blessing of human intelligence, a person's life would be severely limited.

### Thank Hashem for your mind.

בָּרוּךְ אַתָּה ה', אֱלֹהֵינוּ מֶלֶךְ הָעוֹלָם, הַנּוֹתֵן לַשֶּׂכְוִי בִינָה לְהַבְחִין בֵּין יוֹם וּבֵין לָיְלָה:

# "He has not made me a gentile."

- Be grateful that you are a member of the nation that was chosen by Hashem to receive the Torah with its 613 Divine commandments.

- Each *mitzva* is a priceless gift from the Creator, for which we must be eternally grateful. It is as if you win a lottery each time you do a *mitzvah*!

- Your Jewish identity may become concealed, buried, or forgotten. We remind ourselves daily of our unique good fortune.

## Thank Hashem for your identity — being Jewish.

בָּרוּךְ אַתָּה ה׳, אֱלֹהֵינוּ מֶלֶךְ הָעוֹלָם,
שֶׁלֹּא עָשַׂנִי גּוֹי:

**Sefardi women say:**

בָּרוּךְ אַתָּה ה׳, אֱלֹהֵינוּ מֶלֶךְ הָעוֹלָם, שֶׁלֹּא עָשַׂנִי גּוֹיָה:

# "He has not made me a slave."

- We are free to serve Hashem without restrictions and we are obligated to keep all of the Torah's commandments.

- In addition, Hashem freed us from the backbreaking slave labor in Egypt and elevated us to be His chosen nation.

### Thank Hashem for your freedom.

## בָּרוּךְ אַתָּה ה', אֱלֹהֵינוּ מֶלֶךְ הָעוֹלָם, שֶׁלֹּא עָשַׂנִי עָבֶד:

**Sefardi women say:**

בָּרוּךְ אַתָּה ה', אֱלֹהֵינוּ מֶלֶךְ הָעוֹלָם, שֶׁלֹּא עָשַׂנִי שִׁפְחָה:

# "He has not made me a woman."
# / "He has made me [a woman] according to His will."

- Male or female, Hashem designed us to perfection and gave us exactly what we need to achieve perfection in the world.

- Men must thank Hashem for the additional *mitzvos* they have, which are not incumbent upon women (generally those *mitzvos* that depend on a time factor).

- Women are grateful for their unique role as wives and mothers, for which they were specifically created, and for the many *mitzvos* they are obligated to fulfill. Their career and happiness are different from those of men, for they were created by Hashem for specific purposes (see Beraishis 2:18).

**Thank Hashem for your special role in serving Him.**

## The Morning Blessings and Your Gifts From Hashem

# בָּרוּךְ אַתָּה ה׳, אֱלֹהֵינוּ מֶלֶךְ הָעוֹלָם, שֶׁלֹּא עָשַׂנִי אִשָּׁה:

**Ashkenazi women say:**

בָּרוּךְ אַתָּה ה׳, אֱלֹהֵינוּ מֶלֶךְ הָעוֹלָם, שֶׁעָשַׂנִי כִּרְצוֹנוֹ:

**Sefardi women do not say Hashem's Name:**

בָּרוּךְ שֶׁעָשַׂנִי כִּרְצוֹנוֹ:

# "He opens the eyes of the blind."

- The ability to see is a tremendous gift from Hashem, for which we must thank Him.

- The eyelid protects the eyes. Each time the eyelids close, they serve to remind us that sight is a gift.

### Thank Hashem for your eyesight.

בָּרוּךְ אַתָּה ה', אֱלֹהֵינוּ מֶלֶךְ הָעוֹלָם,
פּוֹקֵחַ עִוְרִים:

See page 98.

# "He clothes the naked."

- All the materials that are used for clothing are provided by Hashem, Who prepares all of our needs for us.

- Garments serve a double purpose:

  ◦ They cover us to prevent others and ourselves from seeing what should not be seen.

  ◦ Clothes call attention to the dignity and importance of the wearer.

**Thank Hashem for your clothing.**

בָּרוּךְ אַתָּה ה', אֱלֹהֵינוּ מֶלֶךְ הָעוֹלָם,
מַלְבִּישׁ עֲרֻמִּים:

See page 166.

# "He releases the bound."

- While asleep, a person is immobile, as if tied up.

- Without Hashem's mercy, even while awake one would continue to be unable to even move his hand or foot or even raise an eyelid.

**Thank Hashem for your ability to move.**

בָּרוּךְ אַתָּה ה׳, אֱלֹהֵינוּ מֶלֶךְ הָעוֹלָם,
מַתִּיר אֲסוּרִים:

# "He raises erect those who are bent over."

- In addition to being able to move, a person is provided with the ability to stand upright.
- Upright posture conveys dignity and raises a person closer to Heaven. It also enables us to bow in humility.

**Thank Hashem for the ability to stand upright.**

בָּרוּךְ אַתָּה ה׳, אֱלֹהֵינוּ מֶלֶךְ הָעוֹלָם,
זוֹקֵף כְּפוּפִים:

# "He spreads the earth over the waters."

"Stepping on the ground, one should thank Hashem for preparing this earth upon which one is able to stand" (*Brachos* 60b).

**Thank Hashem for the ground.**

בָּרוּךְ אַתָּה ה׳, אֱלֹהֵינוּ מֶלֶךְ הָעוֹלָם,
רוֹקַע הָאָרֶץ עַל הַמָּיִם:

# "He provides me with all my needs."

- This blessing is associated with the provision of shoes, which enable a person to get around and take care of his needs (*Brachos* 60b).

- Our shoes and all of our other needs, whether of natural materials or of man-made materials, are all prepared and provided for us by the Creator.

- One is required to request of Hashem all of one's needs, because that is Hashem's intention in not providing certain needs — to bring the person to prayer.

**Thank Hashem for your shoes and for providing what you need to live.**

בָּרוּךְ אַתָּה ה׳, אֱלֹהֵינוּ מֶלֶךְ הָעוֹלָם,
שֶׁעָשָׂה לִי כָּל צָרְכִּי:

# "He prepares a person's footsteps."

- Walking (or any type of mobility) is a marvelous gift for which one must be eternally grateful to the Creator.
- Hashem "prepares" a person's footsteps: He prepares events to test us and teach us.

**Thank Hashem for your ability to walk and for preparing life events for your benefit.**

בָּרוּךְ אַתָּה ה', אֱלֹהֵינוּ מֶלֶךְ הָעוֹלָם,
הַמֵּכִין מִצְעֲדֵי גָבֶר:

# "He girds Israel with strength."

- This blessing was said when putting on one's belt (*Brachos* 60b).
- We thank Hashem specifically for providing us with the means to strengthen ourselves.
- In addition, we realize that a person would not be able to overcome temptation if Hashem did not help him (*Kiddushin*).

**Thank Hashem for your strength.**

בָּרוּךְ אַתָּה ה׳, אֱלֹהֵינוּ מֶלֶךְ הָעוֹלָם,
אוֹזֵר יִשְׂרָאֵל בִּגְבוּרָה:

# "He crowns Israel with glory."

- A head covering reminds us that Hashem is above us.
- We should consider our head coverings as royal crowns of glory!

**Thank Hashem for your head covering.**

בָּרוּךְ אַתָּה ה', אֱלֹהֵינוּ מֶלֶךְ הָעוֹלָם,
עוֹטֵר יִשְׂרָאֵל בְּתִפְאָרָה:

See page 198.

# "He gives strength to the weary."

- A person goes to sleep weary and weak, and Hashem awakens him the next morning refreshed and renewed, full of vigor and energy.

- This strength is a G-d-given blessing, a hint of *techiyas hamaisim* (the resurrection of the dead).

- The need for sleep reminds us of our dependence on Hashem.

**Thank Hashem for sleep.**

בָּרוּךְ אַתָּה ה׳, אֱלֹהֵינוּ מֶלֶךְ הָעוֹלָם,
הַנּוֹתֵן לַיָּעֵף כֹּחַ:

# "He removes sleep from my eyes and drowsiness from my eyelids…"

- The Talmud relates this blessing to the washing of one's face in the morning because this helps one feel like a new person.

- The Creator endows us with enthusiasm, which is spiritual energy that a person can use in the service of Hashem.

## "…accustom us to Your Torah…"

- We can overcome the *yetzer hara* only with Hashem's assistance, and we ask Him to help us connect with Him and His Torah.

- We ask Hashem to assist us in developing our passion for Torah and *mitzvos*.

## "…distance us from evil people…"

- We ask Hashem to create an environment in which we can serve Him without interference.

## "Thank You, Hashem… Who bestows good kindnesses upon His people Israel."

- May Hashem bestow on us His benevolent kindnesses.

This concluding blessing summarizes all of the above. Thank Hashem for His endless kindness in all areas of life.

בָּרוּךְ אַתָּה ה', אֱלֹהֵינוּ מֶלֶךְ הָעוֹלָם, הַמַּעֲבִיר חֶבְלֵי שֵׁנָה מֵעֵינַי וּתְנוּמָה מֵעַפְעַפָּי:

וִיהִי רָצוֹן מִלְּפָנֶיךָ ה' אֱלֹהֵינוּ וֵאלֹהֵי אֲבוֹתֵינוּ שֶׁתַּרְגִּילֵנוּ בְּתוֹרָתֶךָ. וְדַבְּקֵנוּ בְּמִצְוֹתֶיךָ. וְאַל תְּבִיאֵנוּ לֹא לִידֵי חֵטְא. וְלֹא לִידֵי עֲבֵרָה וְעָוֹן. וְלֹא לִידֵי נִסָּיוֹן. וְלֹא לִידֵי בִזָּיוֹן. וְאַל תַּשְׁלֶט בָּנוּ יֵצֶר הָרָע. וְהַרְחִיקֵנוּ מֵאָדָם רָע וּמֵחָבֵר רָע. וְדַבְּקֵנוּ בְּיֵצֶר הַטּוֹב וּבְמַעֲשִׂים טוֹבִים. וְכוֹף אֶת יִצְרֵנוּ לְהִשְׁתַּעְבֶּד לָךְ. וּתְנֵנוּ הַיּוֹם וּבְכָל יוֹם לְחֵן וּלְחֶסֶד וּלְרַחֲמִים בְּעֵינֶיךָ וּבְעֵינֵי כָל רוֹאֵינוּ. וְתִגְמְלֵנוּ חֲסָדִים טוֹבִים: בָּרוּךְ אַתָּה ה' הַגּוֹמֵל חֲסָדִים טוֹבִים לְעַמּוֹ יִשְׂרָאֵל:

### Nusach Edot Hamizrach:

וִיהִי רָצוֹן מִלְפָנֶיךָ ה' אֱלֹהַי וֵאלֹהֵי אֲבוֹתַי, שֶׁתַּרְגִּילֵנִי בְּתוֹרָתֶךָ. וְתַדְבִּיקֵנִי בְּמִצְוֹתֶיךָ. וְאַל תְּבִיאֵנִי לִידֵי חֵטְא. וְלֹא לִידֵי עָוֹן. וְלֹא לִידֵי נִסָּיוֹן. וְלֹא לִידֵי בִזָּיוֹן. וְתַרְחִיקֵנִי מִיֵּצֶר הָרָע. וְתַדְבִּיקֵנִי בְּיֵצֶר הַטּוֹב. וְכוֹף אֶת יִצְרִי לְהִשְׁתַּעְבֶּד לָךְ. וּתְנֵנִי הַיּוֹם וּבְכָל יוֹם לְחֵן וּלְחֶסֶד וּלְרַחֲמִים בְּעֵינֶיךָ וּבְעֵינֵי כָל רוֹאַי. וְגָמְלֵנִי חֲסָדִים טוֹבִים. בָּרוּךְ אַתָּה ה', גּוֹמֵל חֲסָדִים טוֹבִים לְעַמּוֹ יִשְׂרָאֵל:

# COMING SOON...

## The Gifts From Hashem
# MORNING BRACHOS

# COMING SOON!

# Gifts From Hashem
# CLASSROOM EDITION

# You are invited
## Spend November 6, 1973 with
# RABBI AVIGDOR MILLER

That Thursday, Rabbi Miller spoke about the Burning Bush, the greatness of Chovos Halevavos; and the importance of Torah study.

And like all his Thursday evening lectures — fortunately — it was recorded. In fact, any of his nearly 1,900 lectures might be the one you've been waiting to hear.

**Lectures, CD's and sets**
Order from SimchasHachaim.com

**The Rabbi Miller SimchaPod**

**Rabbi Miller Hotline: 25 lectures a month**

**Unlimited listening at MillerLegacy Library.org**

## To order: Call 718-258-7400 x103 or visit simchashachaim.com

*A quotation-a-day by Rabbi Avigdor Miller*

## What unique power has Hashem given you?

The freedom to choose (*bechirah*) is truly miraculous. It is the one area in the entire universe in which Hashem has given authority to man.

— *Ohr Avigdor Shaar Habechinah*

# Daily email... Subscribe FREE!
# j.mp/getsimcha